HITLER'S SAMURAI
The Waffen~SS in action

HITLER'S SAMURAI
The Waffen-SS in action

BRUCE QUARRIE

 Patrick Stephens, Wellingborough

© Bruce Quarrie and Patrick Stephens Limited 1986

All rights reserved. No part of this publication may be reproduced, stored in a retrieval system or transmitted, in any form or by any means, electronic, mechanical, photocopying, recording or otherwise, without prior permission in writing from Patrick Stephens Limited.

1st edition February 1983
2nd edition September 1984
1st paperback edition August 1986

British Library Cataloguing in Publication Data

Quarrie, Bruce
    Hitler's Samurai.—2nd ed.
    1. Waffenschutzstaffel—History
    I. Title
    355'.00943   D757.85

    ISBN 0-85059-806-0

Half title *The German eagle presides over the Sigrunes and the SS motto* (81/141/36).

Title spread *PzKpfw VI Tiger of* Das Reich *at the time of the battle of Kursk: note special divisional marking introduced for this operation* (81/143/13A).

Page 6 *A standard 7.92 mm Kar 98k fitted with a ZF 4 telescopic sight* (75/120/5A).

Patrick Stephens Limited is part of the Thorsons Publishing Group.

Printed and bound in Great Britain.

Contents

Introduction to the third edition

'Rarely has an army had to pay such a high price for defeat as the Waffen-SS.' I quoted this statement from the Waffen-SS old comrades' association in the introduction to the last editions of this book, and it remains true. The whole of the Schutzstaffel, from the most richly deserving butchers like Eichmann to the young teenagers of the Hitler Youth who fought with desperation beyond their years in the bloodbath that was Berlin in 1945, was tarred with the same brush: guilty until proven innocent. In this book it has been my intention to give a more balanced view, with particular reference to the SS-VT and Waffen-SS.

I have tried to show what sort of people did join the SS, and why; how they were trained, organised, uniformed and equipped; and, through a précis of their campaigns, what their achievements—good and bad—were. To many people, even today, no Waffen-SS accomplishment can be classed as 'good', but this biased emotional reaction denies the Waffen-SS the same *military* recognition awarded to the élite formations of other nationalities, past or present. It is also a reaction which denies the effect many aspects of Waffen-SS training and uniform have had on all postwar armies, and which are discussed later. Finally, it is a reaction which places the atrocities like Le Paradis and Oradour ahead of the many acts of chivalry performed by SS individuals and units, and which ignores the inconvenient fact that Allied troops—and not just the Russians—were guilty of similar atrocities, including the shooting of prisoners and reprisals on the civilian population of Germany.

The photographs which form this volume's core are the work of SS war correspondents (Kriegsberichter) and have been selected from many thousands in the copious files of the Bundesarchiv in Koblenz, West Germany. To any reader unaware of Bundesarchiv conditions, I must point out that their photo archives are only open to publishers or to individuals working to a publisher's commission; prints cannot under any circumstances be provided for private collectors, model makers or enthusiasts. This is not my ruling, it is the Bundesarchiv's, so please do not write to myself or to the publishers of this book asking for copy prints, because they cannot be made available.

Since writing this book in the first place, I have been deluged with requests from readers for further information in particular about the seven premier Waffen-SS Panzer Divisions: the Leibstandarte *Adolf Hitler, Das Reich, Totenkopf, Wiking, Hohenstaufen, Frundsberg* and *Hitlerjugend*. A sequel is therefore now available entitled *Hitler's Teutonic Knights,* also published by Patrick Stephens, which includes chapters on each of these divisions plus less detailed information on other Waffen-SS formations which contained a Panzer battalion. The book also contains some colour photographs which I was fortunate enough to find in Berlin. I hope you enjoy them as much as their discovery delighted me.

As before, this book is dedicated to the victims of aggression everywhere.

Bruce Quarrie
Wellingborough, March 1986

1. The recruits

What sort of man (or woman) did join the SS? This, I am sure, lies at the forefront of the mind of most people today enquiring into the whole murky issue. The answer, regrettably, is not as simple to give as one might wish, because the million men of the Waffen-SS, and millions of other members of the Allgemeine-SS (including the Sicherheitsdienst, Gestapo and Totenkopfverbände, to name the three most sinister organisations within the NSDAP), included middle and officer class intellectuals as well as illiterate sadists, idealists as well as opportunists, prosperous farmers and industrialists as well as the down-and-out and unemployed, and every shade and variation in between. Moreover, it is vital to draw distinctions between the original Reichsdeutsche volunteers, the later Volksdeutsche recruits, the western European members and the motley rabble of non-Aryan SS troops which included Slavs, Moslems, Cossacks and others, many of whom were impressed or shanghaied into service rather than volunteering in any case.

To take the first group first—German people living within the confines of Germany proper, excluding Austria, Czechoslovakia and the Sudetenland—the first statement which must be made is that not all members of the SS were National Socialists any more than all National Socialists were members of the SS. And here it is wise to pause and examine what 'Nazism' actually meant to the people of Germany in the 1920s and '30s, and its relationship to 'Fascism', since both words have acquired post-war meanings and connotations far removed from their original concepts.

'Nazi' is, today, used as a convenient label to describe any extreme right-wing movement or individual. However, it must not be forgotten that the fledgling Deutsche Arbeiterpartei was first and foremost a working class movement whose emotional roots lay in disillusionment at high unemployment and inflation, in dissatisfaction with contemporary political leadership, in antagonism towards the tenets of communism and in outrage against the provisions of the Versailles Treaty.

Nevertheless, it is not an endearing doctrine to modern minds, although anyone with the advantage of hindsight and the opportunity of seeing what excesses it led to, is in a more privileged position than the 'man in the street' of pre-war Germany.

To summarise as briefly as possible, the main Nazi social and political doctrine is simple: 'race' is the most important single element in society; the German race is superior to all others (and especially to Jews, Slavs and gypsies), so Germany should rule Europe. It is also easy to see why such an extreme doctrine was capable of infecting the minds of so many people in pre-war Germany. The whole country was labouring under a massive inferiority complex caused by its defeat in the First World War (after an unbroken hundred-year run of victories) and the criminally irresponsible reprisals and restrictions imposed by the Allies at Versailles. It wasn't the German people who were responsible for defeat, the

Left *NSDAP rally in the Luitpold Stadium in Nürnberg, 1934. The Leibstandarte forms an honour guard in the foreground, while Hitler, flanked by Himmler and Lutze (then head of the SA), salute. The centre foreground figure is probably Dietrich (ABC-4062A).*

argument ran, but the bolshevik agitators and malingerers, the Jewish profiteers and the incompetent Generals.

Nazism's earliest manifesto, adopted in February 1920, was the '25 Points', which were genuinely both 'socialist' and 'nationalist' in aim. The right to work and the provision of jobs for all was one of the main ingredients—but the other side of the coin was forced labour or imprisonment for the habitually unemployable. Nationalisation of industry and commerce was another of the Party's platforms, and land reform a third. More sinister was the requirement that a strong, central, national government was needed, and one under which full citizenship would only be allowed to those of pure 'Aryan' descent. Curbs on the freedom of the Press were also in the manifesto, along with a demand for the re-establishment of the German armed forces and return of German colonies confiscated at the end of the First World War.

'Fascism' is often confused with Nazism in popular usage, but was an entirely separate Italian movement; ironically, although it, too, was anti-communist in motivation, one of fascism's prime tenets was seizure of factory control by and for the workers. After the First World War its aims became more nationalist in scope, demanding greater respect for Italy in the League of Nations and a stronger form of centralised government. Essentially, 'fascism' is much the same as syndicalism and, although the ambitions of the Italian Fascist Party headed by Benito Mussolini, and the German Nationalsozialistische Deutsche Arbeiter Partei (NSDAP), grew increasingly closer together during the 1930s, people today, who use the terms 'Nazi' and 'fascist' as derogatory synonyms, neither help their own cause nor aid historical understanding.

Having said that, it is unfortunately necessary to admit that neo-Nazi/fascist feeling still runs high, not just in Germany but elsewhere in Europe, including most especially the British Isles. These days, however, other racial groups have taken the place of the Jews, partly as a result of horror at what happened in the German concentration camps, partly because of sympathy for the modern state of Israel, and partly because other nationalities are seen as a 'threat'. Today's 'Nazis', therefore, are those who seek to brand minorities such as the Pakistanis or Irish as the source of our social and economic problems. And it is a sad truism that 'send them back where they belong' is as common a phrase in this country today as it was in Germany half a century ago. Despite this, people are not flocking to join the notorious League of St George, or other neo-Nazi movements today, as the German people flocked to join the NSDAP and the SS in Germany. Despite similar economic problems and a comparable unemployment rate, it seems obvious that the terrible example of Hitler's excesses is holding most people back from following a similar course.

One prominent group of people attracted to the SS in the early days was that comprising former Freikorps men, now unemployed, rootless and looking for an ideal and a leader to restore their self-respect. In this they were identical to the millions of other Germans who succumbed to Hitler's strange magnetism. Where they differed was in an innate conviction that they really were 'superior' and in a desire to belong to an organisation which would not only recognise this supposed quality, but also provide a legal outlet for its expression. Most recruits in this group came from what one can loosely call the lower middle classes of artisans and small businessmen, but the appeal of the SS soon extended throughout the middle and upper middle classes. Here, however, the lure was more based on a return to 'law and order' than to Nazism's spurious racial theories. Underlying the surface motivation in both groups, however, was a desire to regain simple dignity.

Moreover, to these lonely men, brought up in war and not afraid of violence, force seemed the only way to achieve their aims. In this they did not differ from the hordes of predominantly working class men who joined the 'brownshirts', the Sturmabteilung or SA, although by and large those who joined the SS were more intelligent and steeped in *what was then* middle class morality. For one thing, they hated anything which we would call 'bourgeois' in addition to anything remotely 'bolshevik'; but more importantly, they were contemptuous of life and prepared to be totally ruthless in achieving their aims.

Pfeffer von Salomon, head of the SA in the 1920s, is quoted* as saying: 'The sight of a large number of men, both mentally and physically disciplined and co-ordinated, with an obvious or latent will to fight, makes an enormous impression on all Germans . . .'.

*Die Nationalsozialistische Machtergreifung.

The marching columns of the SA and SS, in effect, exerted a hypnotic influence on a large number of Germans, infusing them with a desire to be part of this great movement. Not all, however, were motivated by idealism. Many of Germany's three million unemployed (1930) joined the SA simply in order to acquire a pair of boots and get a square meal once in a while. The SS tried to stay above this, insisting on recruits paying for their own uniforms, but was unable entirely to eliminate the 'gangster' element.

As the SS movement grew by slow stages, the quality of the recruits gradually changed, initially for the better but ultimately for the worse. The whole NSDAP was desperately short of funds, so what the movement needed to attract was men with money. For this, the SS turned to the traditional German officer classes on the one hand, and to industrial magnates and other wealthy businessmen on the other. The latter, by donating to SS funds, were given SS ranks and allowed to wear the distinctive black Allgemeine-SS uniform. Eventually, in fact, this practice became so widespread that it was difficult to avoid becoming, on paper at least, a member of the SS!

To recruit from the officer classes was initially more difficult. Men of this calibre were not going to be attracted by the undisciplined rabble which comprised 90 per cent of SS membership in the early days. Between 1933 and 1935, therefore, after Hitler became Chancellor and reintroduced conscription, some 60,000 men were expelled from the SS, while overtures were made to certain highly respected members of the aristocracy in order to give the SS a new image of class and respectability. Surprisingly, several prominent members of the old German aristocracy responded favourably, including the Grand Duke of Mecklenburg and the Princes of Waldeck and Hesse. By 1938, 12 per cent of SS officers holding Standartenführer rank or higher, came from the military aristocracy.

Under this leadership, the SS began to attract more and more young university-educated men, products of the national Youth Movement, whose only motivation was power. These men, mainly lawyers and economists, tended to drift into the Sicherheitsdienst or the SS-Hauptampt (later to become the Wirtschafts-und-Verwaltungshauptampt, or WVHA), although some volunteered for the fledgling SS-VT (SS-Verfügungstruppe, later

Schutzstaffel standard bearers march rather raggedly around the Luitpold arena in 1934 (ABC-4033).

renamed Waffen-SS). A greater proportion of the SS-VT's officer cadres, however, were middle class soldiers who transferred from the Reichswehr (the small standing army permitted Germany under the terms of the Versailles Treaty).

Another group whose recruitment into the SS was actively encouraged by Himmler, with his quaint rustic ideals, was farmers' sons, and in fact the SS was never entirely to lose its 'rural' flavour (in contrast to the Army and the SA, whose main source of recruits was in the urban areas).

After the 'clean up' of 1933-35, which attempted to rid the SS of outright criminals, homosexuals, alcoholics, the 'professionally unemployed' and anyone who could not prove he had no Jewish blood, standards for admission were tightened. Racial purity, physical fitness, height and the lack of a criminal record became prerequisites for admission. For a period, a man would not even be considered for admission to the Leibstandarte if he had had a single tooth filled! Under these conditions, the supply of acceptable recruits began to dwindle, but many men who *would* have volunteered, and *would* have been suitable, were deterred by Himmler's anti-Christian policies. He tried, but never succeeded, to make the SS an anti-Church body. SS indoctrination included a great deal of virulent propaganda, and many individuals who clung to their beliefs were victimised mercilessly. It is interesting that it was only in the Waffen-SS and the Totenkopfverbände that the numbers of church-goers ever dropped below 50 per cent (to 31 per cent in the latter case), and that two-thirds of the Allgemeine-SS retained their beliefs.

The result was inevitable. In order for Himmler to continue expanding his empire, he would have to lower his standards. Gradually, not just the religious standards nor those pertaining to height and physical fitness were eroded, but the all-important racial criteria as well. There was, however, yet another reason for this.

The Army had always been suspicious of the SS. As the supposed sole arms-bearers of the State, they regarded the creation of armed units within the SS as a betrayal by Hitler. This was almost certainly unintentional, as it is impossible for Hitler (or Himmler) to have forseen or planned the eventual Waffen-SS army of 900,000 men when, in 1934, he gave the Generals his promise. Some writers have hypothesised that Hitler was playing a double game, and allowed the expansion of the SS-VT and the Waffen-SS as a counter to any possible coup by the Army. Certainly in the early stages (pre-1940), this is extremely unlikely, and Hitler bent over backwards in his efforts to appease the Army.

The Army was, in fact, given effective control over recruitment into the SS-VT. Volunteers were sifted, and only approximately a third of those whom the SS would have deemed acceptable were permitted to enter the SS, the balance having to join the Wehrmacht. Moreover, although in time of peace the SS-VT came under the command of the Reichs-führer-SS, Heinrich Himmler, in time of war it would be controlled totally by the Army. As early as 1935, Hitler stated in a secret document that in time of war 'The SS-VT will be incorporated into the Army'. He clarified this three years later in an Order dated August 17 1938 which stated that, in time of national emergency, the SS-VT would be used for two purposes: 'By the Commander-in-Chief of the Army within the framework of the Army. It will then be subject exclusively to military law and instructions; politically, however, it will remain a branch of the NSDAP'; and, 'at home, in accordance with my instructions. It will then be under the orders of the Reichsführer-SS'.

When one considers that the SS began in 1923

Left *Framed by an arch, officer cadets parade on the square at Bad Tölz (81/145/1).*

Right *Recruits march beneath the entrance to the SS Junkerschule at Bad Tölz (81/144/32A).*

with some 200 men, rising to 52,000 in 1933, the Army's suspicion of the armed branch of the SS—which really stemmed from 'Sepp' Dietrich's Stabswache Berlin of 120 men established on March 17 1933—can easily be understood, although in fact the Waffen-SS never grew to exceed ten per cent of the Army's strength. Prior to the reintroduction of national conscription on March 16 1935, the Army had no jurisdiction over recruitment into the armed SS, although at this time it was so small it posed no threat, despite the part the Leibstandarte had played in the 'night of the long knives'—June 30 1934.

During 1933-34, a number of SS 'political action squads' were organised in key cities, and these gradually coalesced into what was to emerge as the SS-Verfügungstruppe. In the spring of 1935, at the time conscription was reintroduced, this comprised the 5,040 men of the 1st and 2nd SS Regiments *Deutschland* and *Germania*, the 2,660 men in the Leibstandarte *Adolf Hitler* and 759 men attached to the two SS officer training schools at Bad Tölz (established October 1 1934 by Paul Lettow with an intake of 54 cadets) and Braunschweig (opened by Paul Hausser in the spring of 1935). These were the only armed SS units the Army 'recognised', but there were, in fact, others, even though the Army refused to acknowledge that membership of these counted as military service.

Principally, these were the Totenkopfstandarten which had been organised from concentration camp guards by Theodor Eicke. Following the Röhm putsch, Eicke had been appointed inspector of concentration camps and commander of the Totenkopfverbände (death's head detachments). He rapidly reorganised the latter into five armed Sturmbanne, No 1 *Oberbayern*, No 2 *Elbe*, No 3 *Sachsen,* No 4 *Ostfriedland* and No 5 *Brandenburg*, totalling 3,500 men (March 1936).

Previous books on the subject of the Waffen-SS have either sought to (a) dismiss any connection between concentration camp personnel and the front-line troops; (b) make an obvious connection between the two; or (c) assert that the whole SS organisation was such a shambles that drawing any hard and fast lines is impossible, while admitting that there was an interchange of personnel.

Pre-war, there was certainly a difference—and not just one of uniform—between the Totenkopf recruits and those of the SS-VT. (Totenkopf personnel wore brown uniforms in contrast to the black of the Allgemeine-SS and grey of the SS-VT.) To qualify to join the Leibstandarte or SS-VT, a recruit had to be at least 5ft 11 in tall (later 6 ft 0.5 in) and between the ages of 17 and 22. To join the Totenkopfverbände, the height restriction was only 5 ft 7.5 in (later reduced to 5 ft 6.7 in) and the upper age limit was 26.

Neither organisation insisted on educational qualifications (before 1938, 40 per cent of SS recruits had only received what we would call primary school education), but recruits had to have clean police records, had to be able to prove their 'Aryan' backgrounds, and had to be in good physical and mental shape. (It is often forgotten that Hitler's

'Aryan Paragraph' imposed racial standards on the Army too, that their recruits also had to satisfy physical standards, and that political indoctrination in National Socialist ideology formed part of the Army's training curriculum.)

Progressively, both younger and older age groups were recruited into all three SS bodies, the younger and more agile going to the fighting formations and the older (or otherwise militarily unsuitable) into the Totenkopf units, where their presence released concentration camp personnel for front line duties. In practice, there was a constant interchange of personnel which accelerated as the war progressed, a fact which not even Paul Hausser, in his post-war writings, has tried to hide or dismiss. The fact that concentration camp guards wore the same uniforms and carried the same pay books as fighting members of the SS is not really the 'incriminating' point some early post-war writers tried to make it out to be. What *is* relevant is that Hitler himself decreed, first in 1938 and then again in 1939, that personnel from the Totenkopfverbände were to be made available as reinforcements for the SS-VT field units on mobilisation.

Comparative strengths—
German Army and armed SS

	Army	SS
1933	100,000	120
1935	295,000	11,959
1939	730,000*	18-23,000
1940	3,706,104	100-150,000
1941	5,000,000	220,000
1942	?	330,000
1943	?	540,000
1944	9,000,000	910,000

*Plus 1,100,000 Reserves.

A final factor which should be borne in mind is that the pre-war concentration camps were very different from the later death camps, and the calibre of the personnel in these years was also different to that of the brutalised sadists who subsequently manned these establishments.

Let us now examine the growth, training and equipment of the premier Waffen-SS divisions prior to the invasion of Russia, when vast changes began to occur which would eventually transform this élite fighting body into something far different.

Hitler's Samurai

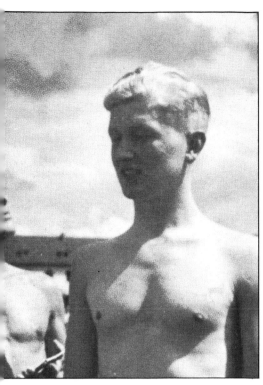

Left *Physical education was an important factor in SS training: cadets on the sports field at Bad Tölz in 1942 (81/145/7).* **This photograph** *Fencing was a very popular sport in the SS, and Heydrich himself was of Olympic calibre (81/144/34A).* **Below left** *More mundane, but also more common, was route marching (81/145/9).*

Above left *Indoctrination. Cadets during a lecture at Bad Tölz (81/145/2).*
Above right, below and right *Then there was the assault course (81/145/5) . . . Weapons training (81/145/3) . . . And hand-to-hand practice (81/145/4).*

Hitler's Samurai

Hitler's Samurai

Above left, left and above *There were endless parades (81/144/35A) ... But congratulations (81/145/10)...And some free time for the survivors (81/145/11). The man on the left of the photo above is Fritz Klingenberg.*

Right *The 'old boy' ... Klingenberg, wearing the Knight's Cross he received in 1941 for the audacious capture of Belgrade, talks to cadets at Bad Tölz in 1942 (81/143/36A).*

Hitler's Samurai

Left *Relaxation at Bad Tölz: senior officials of the Allgemeine-SS join cadets in a wine and music session (81/145/12).*

Below left *A wargames exercise for potential officers from the* Germania *Standarte, most of them wearing NCO insignia at this time, at Bad Tölz (81/145/13).*

Right *A parade of members of the Polizei Division in Vienna in 1941 shows an Oberscharführer with regulation SS insignia in the foreground and men with police collars and, in a couple of instances, helmet badges, in the background (75/120/21A).*

Below *The civilian in the centre of this otherwise uninteresting photo is Professor Ferdinand Porsche, watching a parade of Polizei Division cadets in Vienna (75/120/22A).*

Below right *SS Brigadeführer Walter Krüger and other officers at the same ceremony; it is impossible to see whether or not he is wearing the Knight's Cross, which he was awarded on December 13 1941 as CO of the Polizei Division, but it is probable that this occasion was a celebration. Krüger later commanded* Das Reich *and won the Oakleaves and Swords to his Knight's Cross (75/120/19A).*

The recruits

Paul Hausser wearing the pre-1942 style collar patches of a
Gruppenführer (75/120/32A).

Hitler's Samurai

2. Growth of the Waffen-SS

We have already seen that the Waffen-SS really began on March 17 1933 when 'Sepp' Dietrich established a personal guard for Hitler in Berlin. In September of the same year this body of men was granted the title Leibstandarte SS *Adolf Hitler* and in November they swore a special oath to the Führer himself, placing themselves outside ordinary German military or civil law. Concurrently, the political action squads began to be reorganised along proper military lines to form the nucleus of the SS-VT.

This creation of an élite force, which was and is often compared to the Roman Praetorian Guard or Napoleon's Imperial Guard, began to attract increasing numbers of recruits. Among these was a retired Reichswehr General named Paul Hausser who became to the Waffen-SS what Heinz Guderian was to Germany's Panzer force. A product of the traditional Prussian military school, Hausser had served as a staff officer on both fronts during the First World War and continued serving with the Reichswehr until retiring in 1932, at the age of 52, with the rank of General-leutnant. In 1934 he was approached by Paul Scharfe, the SS judge, and readily accepted the promotion offered from SA Standartenführer to SS Brigadeführer, responsible for the organisation and training of the SS-VT, which up to this time had been handled by the Army insofar as any training was given at all.

Once the two SS officer training schools had been established at Bad Tölz and Braunschweig, Hausser began attracting increasing numbers of former police officials and Reichswehr NCOs into the fledgling SS-VT and, when Hitler established the SS-VT Inspectorate on October 1 1936, Hausser became its head. However, when it came to the actual training programme, the guiding light was really Felix Steiner, who had served as a junior infantry officer in the First World War. Steiner's ideas were quite revolutionary in comparison with the staid and traditional training given to Army recruits, with its emphasis on 'Square bashing'.

During the First World War, as commander of a machine-gun company, Steiner had witnessed the formation of the earliest 'battle groups', in the modern sense of the word. Selected men were withdrawn from the trenches and formed into *ad hoc* assault groups, using individualised weapons which included entrenching tools sharpened like razors, cluster grenades (sticks of four or five grenades tied together) and knuckle dusters. Specially trained for close-quarter fighting, the men of these assault units wreaked havoc in their trench raids, usually carried out at night and without the customary prior notification to the enemy of an artillery barrage.

As a result of his experiences, Steiner, who had been promoted to Captain in the Reichswehr in 1927, was diametrically opposed to the massed ranks of cannon fodder which still characterised most European armies, and believed firmly in the creation of élite, highly mobile groups whose training put the emphasis on individual responsibility and military teamwork rather than mindless obedience.

At the time the two SS officer training schools were being established, Steiner was commander of the SS Standarte *Deutschland*, and had already began putting his theories into practice*. His men

*At a training ground at Dachau, where his men had to share guard duties with the Totenkopf men.

spent more time on the athletics field and in cross-country runs than on the parade ground, developing standards of fitness and endurance which could not be matched by either Army recruits or the members of the Leibstandarte, whom they dubbed 'asphalt soldiers' because of their largely ceremonial role*.

Steiner's reforms gradually permeated throughout the SS-VT hierarchy as their value became recognised; troops who could cover three kilometres in full kit in 20 minutes were unheard of!

Steiner and Hausser had good material to work with. Despite the fact that nearly half the SS recruits

*Not, as is sometimes stated, because of their black uniforms.

had received only minimal education, their stature and fitness were of extremely high standard. Himmler himself boasted, in 1937, that 'we still choose only 15 out of every 100 candidates who present themselves'. Moreover, to be eligible for a commission in the SS-VT, officer cadets had to have served for a minimum of two years in the ranks—which initially, of course, meant in the Reichswehr. Officers enlisted for 25 years (NCOs for 12 and privates for four), and basic training was the same for all groups.

A recruit's day began at 6:00 with a rigorous hour's PT, followed by breakfast of porridge and mineral water—hardly sufficient, one would have

thought, for the hardships to follow! The morning continued with intensive weapons training, target practice and unarmed combat sessions, interrupted three times a week by ideological lectures. A hearty lunch was followed by a comparatively short but intensive drill session, then a period of scrubbing, cleaning, scouring and polishing, and finally a run or a couple of hours on the sports field. If a recruit had any energy left after this, he might be lucky enough to get a pass, but even this involved a close inspection to ensure that every aspect of his uniform was immaculate, that his pockets did not bulge with cigarette packets, wallets, keys or loose change, and that he himself was freshly showered or bathed.

Another innovation introduced by Steiner was designed to break down the rigid divisions between ranks which had always, and still did, exist in the Army. Officers and NCOs were encouraged to talk and mix with their men, to get to know them as individuals; they competed in teams against each other on the sports field; and off duty they addressed each other as *kamerad* (comrade), rather than by ranks.

Once a recruit had finished basic training there was a passing out parade (which was failed by one man in three, first time round) before he was allowed to take the SS oath. The oath was a major ingredient in the SS mystique, binding each successful candidate

The Leibstandarte's reconnaissance troop drawn up on parade on a football pitch, circa 1934; note that their vehicle number plates did not have a Sigrune prefix at this time (ABC-18270).

in unswerving loyalty to the person of Adolf Hitler—not the Party, nor the State. It went as follows[*]:

'I swear to thee Adolf Hitler
As Führer and Chancellor of the German Reich
Loyalty and bravery.
I vow to thee and to the superiors whom thou
    shalt appoint
Obedience unto death
So help me God'.

SS-VT candidates took the oath separately from members of the other SS branches, at 22:00 on November 9 in Hitler's presence at the Nazi shrine before the Feldherrnhalle in Munich. One former SS man remembers[†] the 'splendid young men, serious of face, exemplary in bearing and turnout. An élite. Tears came to my eyes when, by the light of the torches, thousands of voices repeated the oath in chorus. It was like a prayer'.

Prayer or not, this was only the first stage of the SS initiation ceremony. In the SS-VT, the candidate now had to spend a year in one of the SS infantry or cavalry schools, before returning to Munich to swear another oath binding himself to obey Himmler's marriage laws, which were designed to protect racial and physical purity.

More binding than the oaths, in many respects, was the SS motto, and herein lies the reason why I entitled this book 'Hitler's Samurai'.

One of the earliest Europeans to visit, and settle in, Japan, was the great Jesuit missionary, Francis Xavier, in 1549. The meeting was a fruitful one, for the Japanese warrior code of bushido was already very close to that of the Jesuits, the 'storm troopers' of the Counter-Reformation. Both preached unconditional loyalty and obedience. In the Japanese samurai caste, it was a code born of the need for assured fidelity in time of war and, although it especially served the interests of the military class, its tradition of duty and self-sacrifice did benefit the community as a whole. The concept of bushido derived from the earliest days of Japanese history, in which an aristocracy and awareness of birth and rank

had evolved before the first written chronicles, the *Kojiki* and the *Nihonshoki*. It was closely tied in also with the predominant animistic religion, Shinto, which had given ground to Buddhism, imported from China, in the early Middle Ages, but which was enjoying a revival in the 1550s and 1560s under the sponsorship of Nobunaga, the shōgun or warlord, who effectively ruled Japan in the Emperor's name.

Nobunaga welcomed Xavier to his court and a great deal was exchanged between the two—not just ecclesiastical, but also in military and economic matters. However, the relationship was short-lived, for Nobunaga was killed in 1582 and his successor tried to ban all Christians from Japan. This attempt was never wholly successful, although Euro-Japanese relations fluctuated widely for centuries thereafter. What Nobunaga and Xavier had achieved, however, was of lasting import, for the Jesuits effectively tacked the samurai concept of death before dishonour on to their own creed of obedience, creating in different words what—nearly 400 years later—was to become the SS motto: Loyalty is my Honour *(Meine Ehre heißt Treue)*.

Several writers have observed the similarities between the Jesuit organisation and mystique, and that of the SS; and even Hitler referred to Himmler as 'my Ignatius' (Loyola, founder of the Jesuits). The command structures were identical, the doctrine of obedience the same, as was the harsh two-year training period and many smaller details. Even more significantly, both organisations were laws unto themselves, owing no loyalty or obligation to anyone other than Pope or Führer.

Following the marriage oath (which, in fact, Himmler eventually found unworkable—by 1940 he pardoned all those who had broken it, and re-admitted them into the SS), the recruit became a full-fledged SS man and officers of Untersturmführer rank and upwards were given the coveted SS dagger. This was a special mark of distinction permitted only to graduates of the two officer training schools; men who received field commissions were not entitled to it unless they subsequently passed the course.

The dagger was, however, only one of three distinctions which Himmler used as a tool to bind his élite even more closely together. At a lower level, there was the SS signet ring, which was initially supposed to be worn only by those men holding SS numbers below 10,000 (the numbers being tattoed

---

[*] 'Ich schwöre Dir, Adolf Hitler/Als Führer und Kanzler des Deutsches Reich/Treue und Tapferkeit./Ich gelobe Dir und den von Dir bestimmten Vorgesetzen/Gehorsam bis in den Tod/So wahr mir Gott helfe.'

[†] Emil Helfferich, in Heinz Höhne's superb book, *The Order of the Death's Head* (Martin Secker & Warburg, 1969).

in the armpit), but eventually came to be worn by practically every officer after three years' service. But for his favourites, Himmler devised an Arthurian round table which held court in his Wewelsburg castle, and for each of these a coat of arms was devised using runes from German and Nordic mythology.

Once they had received their daggers, SS officers next had to undertake an intensive combat course, which included courage tests such as having to dig a foxhole in front of an advancing tank before it reached you, or removing the pin from a grenade balanced on top of your steel helmet and standing perfectly still while it exploded*. More significant were live firing exercises, with machine-guns, mortars and artillery, which were designed to introduce men of the SS-VT to genuine battlefield conditions and harden them to explosions. Inevitably, there were casualties, and the Army criticised these methods harshly.

However, even John Keegan, author of the best-selling *Face of Battle* and a critic of these methods,

'Sepp' Dietrich awarding Iron Crosses to men of the Leibstandarte following the 1940 campaign in the west (81/144/0A).

admits* that later, 'the rigours of war were to bring to the front a generation of young SS Colonels and Generals whose powers of leadership were perhaps unmatched in the German Army'. In this group are included those whom Gerald Reitlinger describes as 'the SS Generals of legend, starry-eyed, youthful and fanatical'—Fritz Witt, Kurt 'Panzer' Meyer, Fritz Klingenberg, Otto Kumm and others. Such men were vastly different from the real SS butchers like Theodor Eicke or von dem Bach Zelewski—as, indeed, were the older generation of senior officers who had served in the trenches and the Reichswehr, such as Hausser and Steiner, Wilhelm Bittrich and Georg Keppler, who fought well, fought hard and fought with chivalry.

Nevertheless, in the pre-war period the growth of the SS-VT was very slow, due to the lack of Army co-operation and exacting recruitment standards

*G. Reitlinger, *The SS: Alibi of a Nation,* page 78.

Waffen SS: the asphalt soldiers, page 53.

Paul Hausser congratulates Ludwig Kepplinger on his award of the Knight's Cross, September 1940 (75/118/35). Kepplinger was commander of the 11th Company, Der Führer Regiment, at the time. He was killed in action in 1944.

battalion of the Leibstandarte; and in the same year an energetic and Machiavellian 42-year-old, named Gottlob Berger, assumed command of the SS Hauptampt, responsible amongst other duties for recruitment. Berger immediately spotted that three previously untapped sources of manpower were open to SS-VT recruitment: the Totenkopfverbände, the war-time reserves of the same organisation, and a large proportion of the ordinary police (Ordnungspolizei). Meanwhile, Hitler had already agreed to the formation of a third SS-VT Standarte—*Der Führer*, mainly composed of Austrians, and based in Vienna and Klagenfurt. Now, on August 17 1938, a new Führer decree stated that, in time of war, elements of the Totenkopfverbände would reinforce the SS-VT. From these provisions emerged the first four of what were to become known in 1940 as the Waffen-SS divisions: the Leibstandarte *Adolf Hitler, Reich, Totenkopf* and *Polizei*, plus the nucleus of a fifth, *Wiking*. These, particularly the Leibstandarte *AH, Reich* (later *Das Reich*) and *Wiking*, were the premier Waffen-SS formations.

At the beginning of the war the Leibstandarte comprised 3,700 men in four infantry battalions with supporting 7.5 cm infantry gun and 3.7 cm anti-tank companies, plus a pioneer and a motor cycle reconnaissance platoon. The three SS-VT Standarten, *Deutschland, Germania* and *Der Führer*, were each of similar strength and composition. In addition there were five Totenkopf Standarten, of nowhere near the calibre of the Leibstandarte and SS-VT troops: *Oberbayern, Brandenburg** and *Thüringen* (organised from the original five Sturmbanne—see above), plus *Ostmark*, formed in Austria, and *Götze* (later renamed *Heimwehr Danzig*), which was specially formed for the invasion of Poland.

Further expansion followed rapidly in the wake of the Polish campaign. Hitler agreed to the increase of

already discussed. However, a drastic change took place in 1938. Field Marshal von Blomberg, the Minister of War, married a woman who later transpired to have been a prostitute in earlier days. The scandal rocked the High Command and Hitler—who had attended the wedding—had to accept von Blomberg's resignation. At the same time, Reinhard Heydrich, head of the Sicherheitsdienst* since 1932, had prepared what later proved to be a false dossier purporting to show that von Blomberg's logical successor, von Fritsch, was a homosexual. Whether Hitler believed Heydrich's evidence or not, he seized upon it as a golden opportunity to unite the roles of Chancellor and War Minister in one man—himself. On February 4 1938 he declared: 'Henceforth I will personally exercise immediate command over all the armed forces. The former Wehrmachtampt in the War Ministry becomes the High Command of the Armed Forces (Oberkommando der Wehrmacht, OKW) and comes directly under my command as my military staff'.

A month later, when German troops marched into Austria, they were accompanied by a motorised

---

*SS Security Service, responsible for the Sicherheitspolizei, Security Police, which comprised the Geheime Staatspolizei, the dreaded Gestapo, and the Kriminalpolizei, the Kripo.

*It was the 4th Company of this Standarte, under Obersturmführer Knöchlein, which was responsible for the massacre of a hundred British PoWs of the 2nd Royal Norfolk Regiment at Le Paradis on May 27 1940.

Hitler's Samurai

the existing armed SS formations into three divisions, with appropriate supporting services; and to increase the strength of the Leibstandarte, initially to that of a reinforced regiment (May 1940), then, after the summer blitzkrieg, to that of a brigade (August 1940).

The three SS-VT Standarten were brought back to Germany for reorganisation, Eicke's Totenkopf units were similarly expanded and a third division was formed by General-major Karl Pfeffer-Wildenbruch out of, predominantly, Ordnungspolizei personnel—most of whom were neither members of the Nazi party nor the SS!—with a leavening of SS-VT and Totenkopfverbände troops.

Following the campaigns in Norway, Denmark, France and the Low Countries, the energetic Berger devised a new way of expanding his master, Himmler's, Waffen-SS formations (the title had become official on March 2 1940) without violating the OKW restrictions on SS recruitment. In the occupied territories there were many young men bedazzled by the speed and efficiency of the German operations, who had not yet learned the truth of what life was to be like 'under the jackboot', and who shared many of National Socialism's ideals. Himmler had already accepted, as early as 1938, the presence of non-Germans— including Americans, Swedes and Swiss—in the SS. Such men, of Nordic if not Germanic descent, did not offend his racial sensibilities. In September 1940 he said 'we must attract all the Nordic blood in the world to us, and so deprive our enemies of it, in order that never again will Nordic or Germanic blood fight against us'.

The first non-German SS formation to be organised was the Standarte *Nordland*, which contained 294 Norwegian and 216 Danish volunteers plus a substantial 'stiffening' of German and Volksdeutsche recruits. Shortly afterwards, in July 1940, sufficient Dutch and Flemish volunteers were available (630) to form the nucleus of a second battalion, named *Westland*. And at the end of the year the *Germania* Standarte of the SS-VT was attached to these, together with additional reinforcements, to create a new SS division, originally called *Germania*, then *Wiking*.

These Nordic volunteers enjoyed less stringent conditions of service than German recruits, being allowed to join on a 'hostilities only' basis instead of

Growth of the Waffen-SS

for the usual minimum four-year term, and the initial height restriction of 1.65 metres was soon abolished. They received the same pay and wore the same uniforms as members of the regular Waffen-SS, with national distinctions, and were subject to the same laws.

Even this expansion was insufficient once Hitler began seriously planning his invasion of the Soviet Union, first apparently discussed in July 1940 but held in abeyance until it became clear, after Göring's failure to subdue the Royal Air Force in the Battle of Britain, that Operation Seelöwe—the invasion of Britain—was impractical.

Further recruitment of ethnic volunteers from the occupied territories was, therefore, organised. However, the appeal had to be to nationalism rather than to National Socialism, with the defeat of communism as the aim.

The different classes of foreign volunteers swore different oaths to the normal SS oath quoted above.

Cuff title variations. **Below** *A volunteer in the Freikorps Danmark also wearing the insignia of the SS-Schule Tölz.* **Bottom** *A Rottenführer of the 17th SS Panzergrenadier Division* Götz von Berlichengen *(Christopher Ailsby Photographic Collection).*

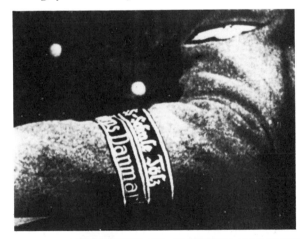

Germanic volunteers prefaced the oath with the words: 'I swear to thee, Adolf Hitler, as Germanic Führer, Loyalty and bravery', the second sentence being the same as in the ordinary oath. Non-Germanic volunteers—for example, Finns—prefaced the oath with the words: 'I swear to thee, Adolf Hitler, as Führer, Loyalty and bravery', etc.

The first unit formed from this new category of recruits was the Freiwilligen (literally, 'free will', ie, volunteer) Standarte *Nordwest*, composed of 2,500 Dutch and Flemish volunteers. Shortly afterwards, this was split into two ethnic battalions, Freiwilligenverband *Niederlande* and Freiwilligenverband *Flandern* and, after the invasion of Russia, these and other legionary volunteers took a new oath, which was significant in that it committed them solely to the Russian campaign: 'I swear by God this holy oath that in the struggle against Bolshevism I will unconditionally obey the Commander in Chief of the German armed forces, Adolf Hitler, and as a loyal soldier I am ready, at any time he may wish, to lay down my life for this oath'. Soldiers taking this oath were regarded as being attached to, but not part of, the 'real' Waffen-SS, regardless of the valour which many of them showed in the field.

By the end of September 1941, *Nordwest* had been disbanded and the two battalions each became legions in their own right. Meanwhile, after prolonged inter-governmental wrangling, several hundred Finns with National Socialist leanings had been allowed to join the Waffen-SS, 400 of them fighting with *Wiking* from the first day of the invasion of Russia. But, in common with many other foreign volunteers, they found that the treatment accorded them by their German instructors and officers was not what they had been led to expect, and by September, again, they had been formed into their own unit, Finnisches Freiwilligen Bataillon der Waffen-SS, although, from early 1942, it became the third battalion of the *Nordland* regiment, within the *Wiking* Division.

Recruits were also trickling in from other occupied territories: into the Freikorps *Danmark*, which was established separately from the *Nordland* regiment; into the Freiwilligen Legion *Norwegen*, and into the Freiwilligen Ersatzbataillon SS, the replacement battalion based outside Graz, in Austria. Such recruits were men who were not willing to join the

SS totally, but were prepared to fight alongside them against bolshevism.

It is important to realise that the *Nordwest* and *Nordland* formations had nothing to do with Kampfgruppe *Nord* (which had been raised in the spring of 1941 from three new Totenkopf Standarten to serve on the Finnish front) and whose morale and training were so bad that they routed and had to be withdrawn for a full year for reorganisation and retraining before being allowed to take to the field again under the grandiose title SS Gebirgs (mountain) Division *Nord*. This was the sixth numbered SS division. Chronologically, the seventh and eighth appear in reverse sequence. No 8, eventually named SS Kavallerie Division *Florian Geyer*, had its beginnings in April of 1941, when an area near Redica in Poland was given over to the training of five then-unallocated Totenkopfstandarten in two Reiter (cavalry) regiments. No 7 was raised by Berger's son-in-law, Andreas Schmidt, in March 1942 from ethnic Germans, mainly Rumanian, in the Balkans. Named SS Freiwilligen Gebirgs Division *Prinz Eugen* it, like *Florian Geyer*, spent most of the war engaged in anti-partisan duties, a form of warfare in which atrocities were bound to occur on both sides—and did. It is important to note, however, that many men who ended up in *Prinz Eugen* and other, later, Balkan SS formations, had little choice in the matter and were either press-ganged by their own governments or by Berger, operating through Heydrich on many occasions. (It is worth also mentioning here, however, in the Balkan context, that Heydrich was assassinated in Prague *not* because of repressive measures against the Czech population, but because he began restoring—albeit in a limited fashion—civil liberties which the British government saw as a threat to the budding resistance movement.)

As the campaign in Russia waxed and waned, consuming millions of lives in the process, the need for manpower to fuel the German war machine gradually overcame Himmler's racial scruples further and further, until ultimately he was prepared to accept virtually anyone other than a Jew into associate membership of the Waffen-SS. In the early days of the campaign, the German soldiers were hailed as liberators by tens of thousands in the Baltic States of Estonia, Latvia and Lithuania; and by the fiercely independent peoples of the Ukraine. Although the Einsatzgruppen (see later) which followed the advancing front line destroyed most peoples' illusions about Nazi benevolence, eventually no fewer than 200,000 assorted Balts, Ukrainians, Russians and even Balkan Moslems would swell the bloated ranks of Himmler's martial empire to nearly a million men.

The greatest expansion period of the Waffen-SS, as the table on page 14 shows, was from 1942-44. Despite severe setbacks during the winter of 1941-42, the German armies rallied back furiously and drove their front line to the far Caucasus. Apart from the *Wiking* Division, as we shall see later, the premier Waffen-SS units took little part in this enormous advance, the LSSAH being involved principally in defensive fighting until withdrawn to France for rest and refit in the summer; *Das Reich*, having suffered very heavy casualties, being withdrawn to Germany even earlier, in March; *Totenkopf* being equally severely mauled in the Demyansk area but staying in the line until early 1943; while the Polizei Division was withdrawn to the Balkans for internal security duties, *Nord* was well occupied in

Men of one of the Totenkopf *regiments in action with a 3.7 cm Pak 35/36 in France, 1940 (the actual date on the photo is May 20) (81/142/10).*

the Finnish sector, and *Prinz Eugen* was still in training. Only *Florian Geyer* accompanied *Wiking*, and then mostly under Army Group Centre and in behind-the-lines anti-partisan duties.

The only new division formed during 1942 itself—and that mainly from 18-year-old German conscripts—was the 9th Division *Hohenstaufen*. However, it took no less than 15 months to work up before being committed to the line, in Poland, in March 1944.

During 1943 another similar German conscript division, *Frundsberg*, was formed, and went into action for the first time as did *Hohenstaufen*. However, during the summer of 1943 the Scandinavian regiments, *Nordland*, Freiwilligen Legion *Norwegen* and Freikorps *Danmark*, were expanded and reorganised into the 11th SS Division *Nordland*. In the spring of the same year the nucleus of the 12th Division *Hitlerjugend*, recruited from 17-year-old Hitler Youth youngsters, had commenced; the 13th *Handschar* was being organised around a cadre of *Prinz Eugen* personnel from Bosnian Moslems; the 14th *Galicische Nr 1*, later renamed *Ukrainische Nr 1*, from 30,000 Ukrainian volunteers; the 15th *Lettische Nr 1* from Latvian recruits, many of whom had served (in the *Schuma*-Bataillon) with the German forces since July

1941; and the 20th *Estnische Nr 1* from Estonian troops.

During the fateful summer of 1943, Himmler's personal escort, Begleit Bataillon Kommandostab *Reichsführer-SS*, was expanded to brigade strength and, by October, that of a division; the 17th Division *Götz von Berlichingen* was raised in France from a variety of replacement and training units, drafts from existing divisions and some Balkans of German extraction; the *Niederland* Legion was expanded to brigade size, as was the *Flandern*, but the latter received the new title *Langemarck*; and the Walloon regiment, *Wallonische* Legion, previously an Army formation, passed to the SS as the nucleus of what would become the 28th Division *Wallonien*.

During 1944 the 18th Division *Horst Wessel* was raised around a cadre of German personnel from Hungarian Volksdeutsche; the 19th, *Lettische Nr 2*, was formed from new Latvian volunteers; the 21st, *Skanderberg*, from Albanian Moslems; the 22nd *Maria Theresia* from more Hungarian Volksdeutsche around a nucleus of *Florian Geyer* veterans; the *Karstwehr* Bataillon, a security unit which had been based in Italy at the time of the armistice in September 1943, was expanded on paper to divisional status (and its name changed to *Karstjäger*), although in fact it only achieved the strength of a weak brigade; and even an Italian 'division' was created, *Italienische Nr 1*, from Fascist security troops.

Of more significance than most of these, however, was the *Charlemagne* Division, *Französische Nr 1*, which, like the Walloon Legion, had originally served as an Army formation before being transferred to the SS in August 1943; and the infamous Kaminski Brigade of renegade Russians and Ukrainians which received the designation *Russische Nr 1*. A second Russian division, *Russische Nr 2*, was formed in 1944, as were a variety of other so-called Waffen-SS units, many of which barely existed except on paper, being comprised of a rag, tag and bobtail assortment of convalescents, stragglers, attempted deserters and other dregs.

However distasteful, it must also be mentioned that German attempts to suborn British prisoners of war into the SS to fight in Russia were not wholly unsuccessful, and that 58 fought in the *Britische Freikorps*. Their leader, John Amery, was later tried for treason at the Old Bailey and executed. (See Appendix 1 for further information.)

A complete listing of Waffen-SS divisions follows, in numerical rather than chronological order. It should be remembered, however, that dozens of other formations existed within the overall Waffen-SS 'umbrella', including the various training schools[*], the ski battalion *Norge* and two SS Fallschirmjäger (paratroop) battalions which were, in fact, penal units, much like the notorious Dirlewanger 'Division'.

1st SS Panzer Division Leibstandarte *Adolf Hitler* (LAH) (Dietrich[1])

2nd SS Panzer Division *Das Reich* (Hausser)

3rd SS Panzer Division *Totenkopf* (Priess)

4th SS Polizei Panzergrenadier Division (Pfeffer-Wildenbruch)

5th SS Panzer Division *Wiking* (Steiner)

6th SS Gebirgs Division *Nord* (Demelhuber)

7th SS Freiwilligen Gebirgs Division *Prinz Eugen* (Phleps)

8th SS Kavallerie Division *Florian Geyer* (Bittrich)

9th SS Panzer Division *Hohenstaufen* (Bittrich)

10th SS Panzer Division *Frundsberg* (Debes)

11th SS Freiwilligen Panzergrenadier Division *Nordland* (von Scholz)

12th SS Panzer Division *Hitlerjugend, (Witt)*

13th Waffen Gebirgs Division der SS *Handschar*[2] *(Kroatische Nr 1)* (Sauberzweig)

14th Waffen Grenadier Division der SS *(Galizische/ (Ukrainische Nr 1*[3]*)* (Shimana)

15th Waffen Grenadier Division der SS *(Lettische Nr 1)* (Hansen)

16th SS Panzergrenadier Division *Reichsführer SS* (Simon)

17th SS Panzergrenadier Division *Götz von Berlichingen* (Ostendorff)

18th SS Freiwilligen Panzergrenadier Division *Horst Wessel* (Trabandt)

19th Waffen Grenadier Division der SS *(Lettische Nr 2)* (Schuldt)

20th Waffen Grenadier Division der SS *(Estnische Nr 1)* (Augsberger)

21st Waffen Gebirgs Division der SS *Skanderberg (Albanische Nr 1)* (Schmidhuber)

---

[*]In addition to Bad Tölz and Braunschweig, officer training schools were later established in Prague, Klagenfurt and Posen Taskau; NCO schools at Lauernberg, Radolfzell, Arnheim, Laibach, Lublinitz, Posen Taskau and Braunsberg; and a variety of specialist training centres throughout Germany, Austria, Czechoslovakia, Poland and other occupied countries.

22nd Freiwilligen Kavallerie Division der SS *Maria Theresia* (Zehender)

(23rd Waffen Gebirgs Division der SS *Kama*[4] *(Kroatische Nr 2)* (Raithel))

23rd Freiwilligen Panzergrenadier Division *Niederland/Nederland*[5] (Wagner)

24th Waffen Gebirgs Division der SS *Karstjäger* (Brandt)

25th Waffen Grenadier Division der SS *Hunyadi (Ungarische Nr 1)* (Grassy)

26th Waffen Grenadier Division der SS *(Ungarische Nr 2)* (Tiemann)

27th SS Freiwilligen Grenadier Division *Langemarck* (Müller)

28th SS Freiwilligen (Panzer[6]) Grenadier Division *Wallonien* (Dégrelle)

(29th Waffen Grenadier Division der SS *(Russische Nr 1)* (Kaminski))

29th Waffen Grenadier Division der SS *(Italienische Nr 1)* (Heldmann)

30th Waffen Grenadier Division der SS *(Russische Nr 2)* (Siegling)

31st SS Freiwilligen (Panzer[6]) Grenadier Division *Böhmen-Mähren*[7] (Lombard)

32nd SS Freiwilligen/Panzer[8] Grenadier Division *30 Januar* (Kempin)

(33rd Waffen Kavallerie Division der SS *(Ungarische Nr 3)*[9])

33rd Waffen Grenadier Division *Charlemagne (Franzosische Nr 1)* (Dr Krukenberg)

34th SS Freiwilligen[10] Grenadier Division *Landstorm Nederland* (Kohlroser)

35th SS Polizei Grenadier Division (Pipkorn)

36th Waffen Grenadier Division der SS (Dirlewanger)

37th SS Freiwilligen Kavallerie Division *Lützow* (Gesele)

38th SS Grenadier Division *Nibelungen* (would have been Lammerding)

39th (?) Gebirgs Division der SS *Andreas Höfer*[11]

40th (?) SS Freiwilligen Panzergrenadier Division *Feldherrnhalle*[11]

41st (?) Waffen Grenadier Division der SS *Kalevala (Finnische Nr 1)*[11]

Theodor Eicke, commander of the Totenkopf *Division, in Russia, 1941. He is wearing a leather greatcoat (81/143/31A). Eicke was killed on February 26 1943 when the aircraft in which he was flying was shot down by a Soviet fighter.*

42nd (?) (SS Division) *Niederschsen*[11]
43rd (?) (SS Division) *Reichsmarschall*[11]
44th (?) SS Panzergrenadier Division *Wallenstein*[11]
45th (?) (Germanische?) SS Division *Warager*[11]
(This was the name originally dreamed up by Himmler for what actually became *Nordland*.)

Notes

[1] The final name in brackets is the name of the first commander of each division, where known; in many cases, change in leadership came almost monthly thereafter.

[2] Those units which were *of* the SS but not part of it have the suffix 'der SS' instead of the prefix 'SS'.

[3] As explained above, the name was changed from *Galizisches* to *Ukrainisches.*

[4] Although recruiting started for this division in June 1944, the speed of the Soviet advance killed it before it got off the ground, and the number '23' was therefore re-allocated. This also happened to the 29th and 33rd.

[5] Acquiring the above numerical designation, the Dutch division's name was spelt in both these ways on its cuff titles.

[6] Some sources merely give 'Freiwilligen', others 'Freiwilligen Panzer' in these units' designations; which is correct may never now be known for certain.

[7] Name attributed by Holzmann (see bibliography) and acknowledged by Windrow but lacking proper documentation.

[8] Here, different sources give 'Freiwilligen' *or* 'Panzer'; as this 'division' was formed largely from human flotsam in Kurmark in January 1945, either designation is as likely on paper as it is unlikely in practice, although no doubt a few men were volunteers and they did possess a few tanks.

[9] No commander's name can be given as this was an *ad hoc* cavalry force apparently raised in Hungary just before the end; it certainly never reached divisional strength, and seems to have fallen apart in Budapest in February 1945.

[10] Some sources delete the word 'Freiwilligen' from this unit's title.

[11] All these units seem to have existed in the imagination only but, assuming they did have more substance than words on paper, would certainly have comprised no more than small groups of stragglers.

Gruppenführer Hermann Fegelein, commander of the Florian Geyer *cavalry division, photographed in 1943 (81/142/19). He was later shot on Hitler's orders after being found, blind drunk, in his Berlin flat following a visit to his field HQ at Hohentychen during the last days of the Russian assault on Berlin. It has been said that he was trying to escape—but in that case, why did he specially comandeer a Ju 52 to fly him back into Berlin when he found he could not return by car?*

Obersturmbannführer Otto Kumm photographed in Kharkov, March 1943 (75/119/33). Kumm at this time was commander of the Der Führer *Regiment and later, as Brigadeführer, became CO of the* Prinz Eugen *Division. He received the Iron Cross First and Second Class during the French campaign, the Knight's Cross in 1942, Oakleaves 1943 and Swords 1945.*

Sturmbannführer Sylvester Stadler, also photographed at Kharkov in 1943 (75/119/31). He later commanded the Hohenstaufen *Panzer Division.*

Obersturmbannführer Werner Ostendorff shortly after winning the Knight's Cross in Russia, September 1941 (75/120/33A). He had been an instructor at Bad Tölz and served on Hausser's staff until taking over command of Götz von Berlichingen *in the west in 1944. He finally commanded* Das Reich *in Hungary, where he was fatally wounded.*

Alfred Wünnenberg, commander of the 3rd SS Polizei Rifle Regiment, in Russia, 1941 (81/146/9A). Notice the police-style collar patches and cap badge. Wünnenberg won the Knight's Cross in 1942 and ended the war as head of the Ordnungspolizei.

Hitler's Samurai

*Obersturmbannführer Manfred Schöufelder, IA of
the 5th SS Panzer Division* Wiking *(81/144/28A).*

*Sturmbannführer Josef Schwörer, supply officer of
the* Prinz Eugen *Division, photographed in 1944
(75/120/14A).*

Left *On the right, wearing the SS-pattern tunic for self-propelled artillery personnel, is an Obersturmführer of the* Wiking *Division. His vehicle is one of many German hybrid tank destroyers, combining a captured Russian 7.62 mm anti-tank gun with a converted PzKpfw II hull and chassis. Note that the NCO on the left is wearing a peaked field cap in camouflage print (81/144/21A).*

Below left *Wilhelm Bittrich, on left, addresses officers of the* Hohenstaufen *Division in France, September 1943. Interestingly, he wears no collar insignia (75/120/11A). Bittrich is best known today for his defeat of the British paratroop force at Arnhem in 1944.*

Above right *Admiral Horthy being greeted by Ribbentrop, Keitel and, on the right Martin Borman wearing SS uniform with his unique white cuff title* (Christopher Ailsby Photographic Collection).

Right *Men of the SS Gebirgs Regiment* Reinhard Heydrich, *a component of the* Nord *Division, in Russia, 1944 (81/141/19).*

Above *Decorations for soldiers of the Legion* Nederland *in 1942 or '43* (81/141/4).

Left *An Unterscharführer of the Legion* Norwegen (81/141/3).

Above right *Parade by men of the Freikorps* Danmark *in 1941* (81/143/35A).

Right *A marksman of the 15th Waffen Grenadier Division der SS* (Lettisches Nr 1) *in Russia, 1943* (81/142/36).

3. Uniforms and insignia

This enormous subject is extremely well covered in the Bender-Taylor books listed in the bibliography, so only a précis will be given here.

Headgear

Officers wore a smart black peaked cap with white piping, twisted aluminium cords and an aluminium death's head device on a velvet band beneath the SS variant of the national eagle on the crown. After the introduction of field grey for the armed SS, the cap became field grey with black band and leather peak. A variant for NCOs, also worn by many officers in the field, had a grey cloth peak.

Field caps were of two basic types, both of which appeared, however, in several different styles. These were the boat-shaped Feldmütze and, from 1943, the almost universally worn Einheitsmütze a soft, peaked cap based on the Army's Gebirgsjäger pattern. The Feldmütze, first in black then in grey, originally had a death's head button on the front and the national eagle, on a black triangular patch, sewn to the left side. By the beginning of the war, however, the eagle had been moved to the front of the cap, above the death's head button or cloth badge. Piping was initially in white but, from the end of 1939, NCOs and other ranks were ordered to adopt the Army's arm-of-service (waffenfarbe) colouring (see below).

The Einheitsmütze had a broad flap which was normally fastened at the front with two buttons, but

Left *Obersturmführer Fritz Rentrop, who won the Knight's Cross as CO of the* Das Reich *Division's 2nd Flak Abteilung in October 1941. He was captured and executed by the Russians in February 1945 (75/119/12).*

which could be folded down and buttoned under the chin to protect the ears in cold weather. It was initially issued in grey (black for Panzer troops), but a tropical version in yellow became available later, together with a simplified version, lacking the flap, in camouflage printed cloth. (Some officers had camouflaged versions privately tailored, with the flap.) The death's head device, initially in the form of a woven badge, but later in a cheaper printed form, was sewn to the crown, and the national eagle (or, in the case of the 6th and other mountain divisions, the Gebirgsjäger Edelweiss device) was sewn to the flap on the left side.

Armoured car personnel in the SS-VT wore the Army's early armoured troop crash helmet-cum-beret, in black, with the national eagle above a death's head device on the front. Moslem members of the appropriate Waffen-SS divisions wore their traditional fez, in either field grey or dark red, with the eagle and death's head sewn to the front.

In combat, the Army's Stalhelm, or steel helmet was worn. Initially this was of the ugly 1916 pattern, but by the beginning of the war this had been replaced by the normal 1935 pattern. Initially painted black, and later grey, the helmet had a white shield bearing the SS runes in black on its right side and the normal black swastika in a white circle within a red shield on the left. (In the Polizei formations, this national badge appeared on the *right*, with the police badge, in white on a black shield, on the left.) When the SS-VT adopted their unique camouflage smock (see below), helmet covers made of the same material were also issued. Later, a fringed face mask, clearly seen in one of the photographs, also became available for snipers. Improvised camouflage materials used in the field included chicken wire and string mesh, into which foliage could be inserted. During the winter, helmets were usually whitewashed but a white cloth cover is also often seen.

Black service dress

Pre-war, and sometimes later by officers on leave or during ceremonial events, the SS-VT and Leibstandarte wore the black Allgemeine-SS uniform, comprising a single-breasted tunic with four aluminium buttons down the front, pleated and buttoned breast pockets and sloping button-down hip pockets. The collar was edged with white and black piping (aluminium for officers). A Nazi brassard was worn on the left sleeve. Officers wore white shirts, NCOs and other ranks brown, both with black ties. Black trousers were tucked into standard black Army-pattern marching boots ('jackboots'). A black cap or steel helmet (see above) and black leather belts with SS buckles were worn, except in the Leibstandarte, who had white ceremonial equipment.

Service tunics and trousers

A field grey tunic of the same cut was issued to the SS-VT in 1935, and a simplified version without the deep cuffs, and with a smaller standing collar, in 1937. Cuff titles (see below) were worn on the lower left sleeve, with the national eagle on the same sleeve, between the shoulder and elbow. Collar patches and shoulder boards are discussed separately.

When the title Waffen-SS was adopted in 1940, members of the Leibstandarte, SS-VT and *Totenkopf* formations began to receive the standard Army-pattern field grey tunic, with five buttons down the front and patch pockets on the hips as well as the chest. The pocket flaps were initially scalloped in shape, but this soon changed to a simpler straight-cut design. Later, a tropical version, in lightweight linen of the golden Luftwaffe colour rather than the greenish shade of yellow used by the Army, also became available. Towards the end of the war, a

Three SS soldiers in Russia wearing the camouflage mottled version of the late war tunic. No other identifying insignia are visible (81/144/6A).

Hitler's Samurai

lightweight drill version of this tunic was also made. It was reversible, one side being printed in camouflage patterns, the other side reed green. The brown and white shirts gradually became replaced, at least in the field, by grey ones for both officers and men.

Later, in 1944, wartime shortages forced the introduction of a much simplified combat blouse, modelled on British Army battledress. Made of coarse serge, this had five buttons down the front and two simple patch pockets on the chest. Versions in camouflage material, both SS pattern mottle and commandeered Italian cloth, were also issued.

Members of Waffen-SS armoured car and, later, self-propelled gun and tank units, wore a version of the Army's smart black double-breasted Panzer blouse, with a smaller, more rounded collar, and tapering black trousers with ankle boots. Later, from 1941, self-propelled gun crews received tunics and trousers of the same cut but in grey material. Camouflage-patterned and reed green twill versions appeared late in the war.

White summer walking out tunics and trousers were also issued. These were of Luftwaffe pattern, the officers' tunic having eight buttons and four pleated and scalloped patch pockets, the NCOs' and other ranks' tunic resembling the Fliegerbluse, a short, deeply waisted and pocketless garment with four buttons.

Shirt sleeve order was also permitted in the field, with the collar either buttoned or unbuttoned and sleeves rolled up or down. No insignia was officially supposed to have been worn on the shirt, but eagles, rank badges and even shoulder boards were commonly seen.

Badges and insignia

Collar patches Lozenge-shaped patches were worn on both sides of the collar by all SS-VT and Waffen-SS personnel. These differed significantly from unit to unit, as follows. The Leibstandarte SS *Adolf Hitler* wore plain black lozenges with silver or white SS runes on the right and ranking (see below) on the left. The three SS-VT Standarten *Deutschland, Germania* and *Der Führer* wore the same with the addition of the small numbers 1, 2 and 3 respectively after the runes. Members of the SS-VT signals and pioneer formations wore a lightning flash and crossed pickaxe and shovel respectively to the right of the runes. Members of the *Totenkopf* Standarten, and

later, Division, wore a death's head device on the right. To begin with, Polizei units wore green patches with police-style two-barred braid, on *both* collar sides, but later adopted the SS runes and ranking system.

Members of the following divisions wore SS runes on the right and rank distinctions on the left: *Wiking, Nord, Florian Geyer, Hohenstaufen, Frundsberg, Nordland*, Hitlerjugend, Reichsführer-SS, Götz von Berlichingen, Albanisches Nr 1*, Niederland*, Karstjäger, Hunyadi, Ungarisches Nr 2, Langemarck*, Russisches/Italienisches Nr 1*, Böhmen-Mähren, 30 Januar, Ungarisches Nr 3, Landstorm Nederland*, Lutzow* and *Nibelungen.*

In the case of the asterisked units, variations from the SS runes are known to have existed and are illustrated, together with the collar patch insignia of all other divisions. It should be noted that further variations still did exist on paper and may have actually been manufactured, but no photographic evidence has yet come to light to prove their use.

Ranking insignia on the left-hand collar patch followed a very simple system. An ordinary SS private's patch was plain black, a Sturmann's had a thin double line of white piping on the fore edge and a Rottenführer's, two. An Unterscharführer had a single pip in the centre of the patch, a Scharführer a pip and a line of piping; an Oberscharführer had two pips, a Hauptscharführer two pips and a line and a Sturmscharführer two pips and two lines. The collar patches of ranks from Untersturmführer upwards were outlined in aluminium braid, with distinctions as follows: Untersturmführer, three pips, Obersturmführer three pips and a line, Hauptsturmführer three pips and two lines; Sturmbannführer four pips and Obersturmbannführer four pips and a line. Higher ranks still had oakleaf insignia on *both* collar patches (no SS runes). A Standartenführer had one oakleaf, an Oberführer two and a Brigadeführer two plus a pip (from 1942, three oakleaves and no pip); a Gruppenführer had three oakleaves (plus a pip from 1942) and an Obergruppenführer three plus a pip (two pips from 1942). When the rank of Oberstgruppenführer was introduced in 1942, it had three oakleaves and three pips. This was the highest rank achieved by a Waffen-SS officer.

Collar braid Tresses, 8 mm wide, in silver-grey, were worn round the collar by all NCO ranks from Unterscharführer to Sturmscharführer.

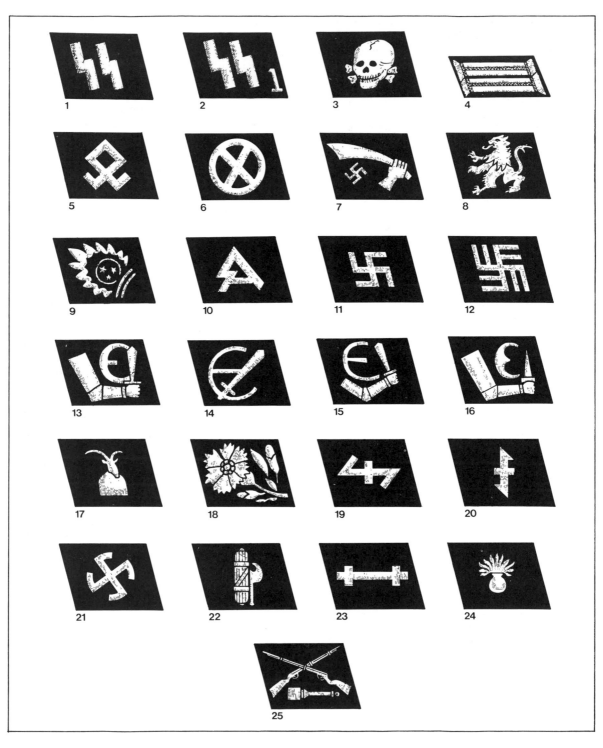

Left 1 *Standard SS runes as worn on right collar patch.* 2 *Variation, Standarte* Deutschland. 3 *Totenkopf.* 4 *Polizei.* 5 Prinz Eugen. 6 Hermann von Salza. 7 Handschar. 8 Galizische Nr 1. 9 Lettische Nr 1. 10 Horst Wessel. 11 Lettische Nr 2. 12 *Worn by members of the armed forces (including Waffen-SS) transferred to concentration camp duties.* 13-16 Estnische Nr 1 *variations.* 17 Albanische Nr 1 *variation.* 18 Maria Theresia, *also worn by one regiment in* Florian Geyer. 19-20 Niederland *variations.* 21 Nordland *variation.* 22 Italienische Nr 1 *variation.* 23 Russische Nr 2. 24 Landstorm Nederland *variation.* 25 Dirlewanger *(reputed).*

Shoulder boards These had a black base and arm-of-service colour (waffenfarbe) piping). The shoulder boards of ranks from private to Rottenführer were otherwise unadorned. An Unterscharführer's had its inner sides edged with 8 mm tresse. A Scharführer's had the outside edge also lined with tresse, as did the next three NCO ranks; in addition, an Oberscharführer had a single pip, a Hauptscharführer two and a Sturmscharführer three. Ranks from Untersturmführer to Hauptsturmführer had the black base covered with silver-grey cord, with the addition of one (Obersturmführer) or two (Hauptsturmführer) pips. Ranks from Sturmbannführer to Standartenführer had silver entwined cords on a waffenfarbe patch on the black base, with the addition of one and two pips respectively for Obersturmbannführer and Standartenführer; pips were originally gold, changed to silver in 1942. An Oberführer's shoulder boards were the same as a Standartenführer's but had a solid waffenfarbe underlay. Higher ranks had entwined gold and silver cords on a silver-grey base, with one central silver pip for Gruppenführers, two for Obergruppenführers and three for an Oberstgruppenführer.

Additionally, the original SS units had Gothic regimental cyphers on their shoulder boards: *LAH* for the Leibstandarte *Adolf Hitler*, D for *Deutschland*, G for Germania and *DF* for *Der Führer*, while the original *Totenkopf* Standartene had numerals. Staff at the two officer schools wore the cyphers *JST* (Junkerschüle Tölz) and *JSB* (Braunschweig). Finally, medical officers wore the traditional Aescapalian staff on their shoulder boards.

Arm-of-service colours (Waffenfarbe) Worn around the shoulder boards by ranks from private to Hauptsturmführer; as shoulder board underlay by ranks from Sturmbannführer to Oberführer; as

piping on headgear for NCOs and men (and unofficially sometimes by officers, instead of their regulation white); and, uniquely, around their collar patches by SS-Panzer Regiment Nr 5 *(Wiking).* The colours indicated at a glance what the wearer's occupation was, and were as follows:

Infantry, all Totenkopf personnel and divisional officers—white; Panzer and anti-tank troops—pink; Panzer engineers—black and white; Artillery—red; Pioneers—black; Cavalry—yellow-gold; Signals—lemon yellow; Reconnaissance troops—copper; Transport troops—pale pink; Supply troops—light blue; Medical personnel—cornflower blue; Gebirgstrüppen—green; Feldgendarmerie—orange; and Rocket troops—wine red.

NCO chevrons A Sturmann had a single V-shaped chevron of 8 mm tresse on a triangular black patch, a Rottenführer a double V; worn on the upper left sleeve, below the national SS-pattern eagle.

National eagle This was worn on the upper left sleeve by all ranks.

Specialist badges Introduced in 1942, these were diamond-shaped black badges with silver-grey devices worn on the lower left sleeve above the cuff title, where applicable. Examples are the Aescapalian staff for doctors and dentists, a lightning flash for signallers, a cogwheel for technical officers, a crossed rifle and machine-gun for armourer NCOs, a harp for bandmasters and a horseshoe for farriers. Other such badges were mainly for administrative, economic and legal officers and thus outside what I consider the scope of this volume.

Cuff titles Most Waffen-SS troops wore a cuff title of one sort or another, either to denote a unit or specialist task, such as Feldgendarmerie (military police) or Kriegsberichter (war correspondent). Several of these are illustrated in photographs. Divisional cuff titles carried the following lettering: Leibstandarte *Adolf Hitler*—*Adolf Hitler* in sütterlin script; *Deutschland, Germania, Der Führer* and *Das Reich*—full title in Gothic script; *Totenkopf*—a death's head; *Polizei*—the words *SS-Polizei-Division* in Roman or Gothic lettering; *Wiking*—Roman or Gothic lettering; *Nord*—Roman lettering; *Prinz Eugen*—Roman lettering; *Florian Geyer* (and *SS-Kavallerie-Division*)—in Roman lettering; *Hohenstaufen, Frundsberg* and *Nordland*—all in Roman lettering; *Hitlerjugend*—in sütterlin script or Roman lettering; *Reichsführer-SS, Götz von Berlichingen*

Good news for a change? An SS war correspondent wearing both the Kriegsberichter and the Leibstandarte Adolf Hitler *cuff titles (and monogrammed shoulder straps) listens to a radio bulletin (81/143/34A).*

and *Horst Wessel*—all Roman lettering; *Skanderberg, Nederland/Niederland, Langemark, Wallonien, 30 Januar, Charlemagne, Landstorm Nederland* and *Dirlewanger*—all in Roman lettering.

In addition, the following cuff titles are all known to have been issued to smaller units, and some are shown in the photographs: *Michael Gaßmair* and *Reinhard Heydrich* (in *Nord* Division); *Norge, Danmark* and *Herman von Salza* (in *Nordland* Division); *General Seyffardt* and *De Ruiter* (*Niederland* Division); *Freikorps Danmark; Frw Legion Flandern; Legion Norwegen; Frw Legion Niederland; Finnisches Frw Bataillon der Waffen-SS; Britisches Freikorps;* and *Ostturkischer Waffen-Verband der SS.*

Cuff titles were 28 mm wide, black with silver-grey edging, and the lettering machine-embroidered in silver-grey. They were worn 14.5 cm above the left cuff. Two have been seen (see photos) worn simultaneously. The three original SS-VT Standarten *Deutschland, Germania* and *Der Führer* had green, blue and red edging respectively to their cuff titles up to the outbreak of war.

National badges Members of the foreign legions frequently wore a national badge, eg, the Union Flag for men in the *Britisches Freikorps*, in the shape of a shield immediately below the national German eagle or just above the cuff title.

Camouflage clothing Obviously, the wearing of normal insignia on camouflage smocks would have ruined the whole effect, so a system of special rank distinctions, adapted from that used on their camouflage smocks by Fallschirmjäger, was devised. These were black rectangular patches with green distinctions for all ranks up to Oberführer, yellow for higher-ranking officers. One to five horizontal green bars were worn by ranks from Unterscharführer to Sturmscharführer; one to three bars with an oakleaf spray by Untersturmführer to Hauptsturmführer; one to four bars with two oakleaf sprays by Sturmbannführer to Oberführer; one, two and three yellow bars beneath a yellow oakleaf spray by Brigadeführers, Gruppenführers and Obergruppenführers respectively; an Oberstruppenführer might have had a single oakleaf spray above a broader single yellow stripe on which were three silver pips, although it is doubtful such a device was actually worn in practice.

Rune breast badge This small diamond-shaped badge in grey containing the SS runes, or Sigrunes, in white, was worn beneath the left chest pocket of the tunic by Reichsdeutsche and Volksdeutsche members of the SS serving in those divisions where no SS runes were worn on the collar patches.

Camouflage and protective clothing

The smock This garment was unique to members of Waffen-SS formations and men of the *Hermann Göring* Division—who adopted many other peculiarities of dress from the Army, Luftwaffe and SS, which are covered in my Osprey/Vanguard* book on the subject. It is the most distinctive Waffen-SS item of clothing and the one most illustrated in the photographs. The smock was a loose-fitting, hip-length garment of lightweight material designed for concealment rather than warmth or other protection from the elements. It had no collar, was drawstringed down the front, drawstringed or elasticated at the waist, and elasticated or, later, buttoned at the cuffs. Early smocks had simple slits above the waistband to allow the wearer to reach pockets or weapons underneath; later versions had button-down flaps over these or integral pockets in the same position.

The most unusual feature of the Waffen-SS smock was the camouflage pattern itself, in an almost bewildering array of mottles combining light, dark

*Fallschirmpanzerdivision Hermann Göring.

Hitler's Samurai

and dusty greens, pink, mauve, brown and russet to blend in with the spring, summer or autumn leaf colours. The smocks were reversible, each side being printed in a different colour combination—including white for winter wear.

Loose-fitting overtrousers in the same materials were also issued but less commonly worn, and not necessarily in the same combination of colours at the same time!

The suit As mentioned above, the standard pattern tunic and trousers were also manufactured, from 1944, in camouflage material of a shoddy nature, as were armoured vehicle crew pattern garments. These also appeared in reed green twill.

Helmet covers Were also produced in camouflage material as noted above.

The one-piece coverall Produced from 1943 in mottle camouflage, this was a loose-fitting 'boiler suit' with two chest and two trouser pockets, designed for AFV personnel.

The two-piece coverall See 'The suit' above. Lapels were smaller than in the standard black or grey AFV tunics.

Anoraks Foreshadowing the parkas issued to the troops of most nationalities today, these hooded garments with two diagonal button-down hip pockets, were either mouse grey or white in colour with fur lining or reversible camouflage-printed with blanket material interlining. Trousers with two thigh pockets were available to match them.

Greatcoats SS-VT personnel had a smart black double-breasted coat with two rows of six buttons down the front. Later, the standard Army-pattern greatcoat in field grey, with collar and shoulder board distinctions as well as cuff titles, sleeve eagles and other insignia, was worn. Officers frequently had fur collars attached or wore privately tailored black leather garments of similar cut. A waistbelt was usually worn by officers and men.

Snow camouflage In addition to the reversible smocks and anoraks referred to above, Waffen-SS personnel, particularly in the *Das Reich* Division, are often photographed wearing loose smocks and helmet covers which appear to have been improvised from sheets. This was probably a common practice, particularly during the first Russian winter 1941-42.

Sniper masks Described under headgear above, but best appreciated by reference to the photographs on pages 120-121.

Anything for warmth! The man on the left has his camouflage smock above a fur coat, complete with shaggy collar. The despatch rider on the right wears the standard rubberised motor cyclists' coat plus a balaclava helmet underneath his field cap which, although partially obscured by his goggles, can be seen to be pulled down square and very tight on his head (75/119/1A).

U-boat clothing Worn by members of SS-Panzer Regiment 12, *Hitlerjugend*, in Normandy in 1944. Two-piece black leather outfit which must have been extremely uncomfortable in hot weather.

Motor cycle coats Double-breasted ankle-length garments of rubberised fabric with two thigh pockets and a deep pleated yoke at the back, these were worn by despatch riders and Feldgendarmerie motor cyclists in all branches of the German armed forces. The skirts contained buttons and buttonholes, enabling them to be fastened at the ankle as over-trousers.

Gebirgsjäger clothing Worn by the Waffen-SS mountain divisions, this was identical to standard Army Gebirgsjäger dress, and included the windproof anorak with single large chest pocket, cleated climbing boots, etc. For further details see my earlier title *German Mountain Troops*, also published by Patrick Stephens Ltd.

Fallschirmjäger clothing The small SS Fallschirmjäger units wore standard paratroop smocks and other clothing, including helmets, but with SS rank distinctions. The rumoured existence of a paratroop smock in SS-pattern mottle camouflage has never been proved, photographically or otherwise.

Other clothing Sheepskin coats and anoraks, fur-lined garments of all kinds, 'liberated' or privately tailored overcoats and virtually anything else which would keep one warm during the Russian winters are all a matter of photographic record.

Tropical clothing

Apart from the rare garment illustrated opposite, the Waffen-SS wore Army and Luftwaffe clothing with SS insignia. These differed slightly in cut and significantly in colour (when new, as both faded to a bleached off-white in the sun and following repeated washings), the Luftwaffe colour being more golden in colour than the Army's greenish shade. The Italian Sahariana tunic, almost identical to the Army pattern, was also worn. Badges and other insignia which were normally silvery in colour were instead either pale copper or rust brown in shade. Tropical topees were occasionally worn, as illustrated, alongside Afrika Korps-style caps.

Footwear

The most commonly seen footwear is the standard Army pattern black marching boot, popularly known as the 'jackboot'. In addition, short black lace-up ankle boots, and Afrika Korps-style long and short desert boots, were common. Heavy felt boots with thick soles were worn during Russian winters. Officers frequently wore black riding boots. Members of SS Gebirgsjäger formations wore Army pattern cleated mountain boots, while those of Fallschirmjäger units wore jump boots.

Belts and buckles

Belts for all ranks were of black leather (except in the Leibstandarte, where white pipeclayed equipment was worn for ceremonial purposes). Officers either had a plain two-pronged white metal buckle, or a clasp and locket buckle, also in white metal, with a circular centre. In this, an eagle clasping a wreath surrounding a vertical swastika surmounted a scroll bearing the SS motto in Gothic script. NCOs and other ranks had a plain rectangular metal buckle with a similar device in its centre, the motto in this case being followed by an exclamation mark. 'Y' strap 'D' ring equipment belts were Army pattern. The standard ammunition pouches, entrenching tool, gas mask container, water bottle and bayonet were all worn. Full marching order included a pack containing blanket roll, greatcoat, tent quarter (see below) and other personal items, including food and spare clothing.

The tent quarter (Zeltbahn)

This extremely useful item was a triangle of reversible waterproofed cloth with a slit down its centre fold, allowing it to be worn as a poncho, and with loopholes around the edges; two or more could thus be looped together to form a windbreak or tent.

Other items

Aiguilletttes Made of aluminium wire, these were worn by officers and adjutants on ceremonial occasions and by Orderly NCOs and NCOs on guard duty.

Gorgets Made of steel, these were worn by Feldgendarmerie, standard bearers and provosts while on duty.

Right Front and rear views of the rare Waffen-SS tropical tunic, which incorporated a Sahariana-style yoke and is known to have been worn in the summer of 1943 by men of the Sturmbrigade Reichsführer-SS on Corsica (Robin Lumsden).

Below right Tropical kit: two NCOs of the Leibstandarte wearing solar topees in Greece, 1941. Note the monogram shoulder insignia (81/141/24).

Daggers and swords Normally only worn for ceremonial occasions. The dagger was basically a German hunting knife with a black handle decorated with the SS runes and an eagle plus swastika wreath; its blade was etched with the SS motto. Swords were straight with black grips bound by aluminium wire, and with nickel-plated guards. They had silver SS runes on the front of the grip. Sword knots were woven aluminium and black silk.

Flags and standards These broadly followed two designs, the Roman 'Vexillum' pattern with a horizontal flag suspended on a crossbar from its pole; and the normal German infantry or cavalry pattern dating back to the days of Frederick the Great. 'Vexillum'-pattern standards only appear to have been awarded to the pre-war formations. A gilt eagle surmounted a swastika wreath at the top of the pole, beneath them a metal plate embossed silver on black giving the name of the regiment. The flags themselves were identical, being red with red, white and black tassels, containing a black and white swastika within a central white circle. Above the central device were capital letters spelling 'DEUTSCHLAND' and below it the word 'ERWACHE' (awake or aware), in white with black edging. Instead of a name on the upper plaque, Totenkopf Standarten merely had a death's head device flanked on either side by the regimental number, in Roman numerals.

Later flags of the German pattern were carried at battalion, squadron or battery level. Infantry and artillery flags were square, cavalry ones of the traditional two-pronged guidon shape. The ground colour was the appropriate arm-of-service (waffenfarbe) shade. In the centre was a Balkan cross with a swastika in the middle and the date 1939 at the foot, in black and white. The corners were filled by national eagle/swastika/wreath symbols, the eagles' heads pointing inwards.

Uniforms and insignia

Although not a member of the Waffen-SS as such, Reinhard Heydrich here displays the elegance of the officers' tunic, the rank insignia of a Gruppenführer, his assorted medal ribbons, the SS sleeve eagle and other details of cut and style to perfection—exactly as one might have expected from this enigmatic perfectionist (69/54/16).

Although the detail is less clear, this portrait of Herbert-Ernst Vahl shows the post-1942 pattern of Brigadeführer collar patches worn on the black SS-style Panzer jacket. Vahl, who only transferred to the Waffen-SS in 1942, after having commanded various Army tank units, became one of several commanders of Das Reich before being appointed Inspector-General of SS Panzer forces. He was killed in a car crash in Greece in July 1944 (75/118/24).

Obersturmführer Erwin Meierdress, commander of
an assault gun battery in the Totenkopf Division, was
photographed here on the hospital steps while recover-
ing from the wounds which won him the Knight's
Cross on March 13 1942. He wears the SS-style self-
propelled gun crew jacket with, as per divisional style,
Totenkopf devices on both collar patches, ranking
being determined by the shoulder boards alone.
Meierdress was killed in action in January 1945
(75/120/13A).

Sturmbannführer Günther-Eberhard Wisliceny looking delighted at the news that he has been awarded the
Knight's Cross for his bravery during the battle of
Kursk while commanding a Panzergrenadier unit in
Das Reich. He later won the Oakleaves and Swords as
well. Note the Army-style waffenfarbe chevron on the
front of his field cap (81/143/15A).

Hauptsturmführer Hans Weiss, who won the Knight's Cross while commanding Das Reich's *reconnaissance battalion during the battle of Kharkov in March 1943. He wears the SS self-propelled gun crew jacket with appropriate insignia and the 'old style' cap with soft crown and peak (75/119/35).*

Hauptsturmführer Vincenz Kaiser, commander of the 3rd armoured battalion, Der Führer, *who also won the Knight's Cross at Kharkov. Note the four badges on his right sleeve denoting single-handed tank 'kills' (75/119/34).*

Unpublished since it first appeared in wartime German newspapers, this photograph is taken from a sequence showing Otto Skorzeny on the day he received his Knight's Cross following the daring Gran Sasso raid to rescue Mussolini. Skorzeny had really wanted to join the Luftwaffe but was prevented from flying because of his size and weight. He won respect on both sides and convinced the jury at Nürnberg that if he was convicted for war crimes, all Allied paratroops and Commandos should be too. During the Ardennes offensive, he commanded 150 Panzer Brigade, which used German tanks disguised as Allied vehicles (81/142/18).

Obersturmführer Heinz Macher, who was awarded the Knight's Cross following the battle for Kharkov in March 1943 while commander of the Deutschland Regiment's pioneer company (81/143/17A).

Wearing the black Panzer jacket with officer's piping around the collar is Untersturmführer Karl-Heinz Worthmann, who won the Knight's Cross during the battle for Kharkov in March 1943; this photograph was taken later in the year, around the time of Operation Citadel (81/143/2A).

Giving a particularly good overall view of NCO insignia here is Hauptscharführer Alois Weber of the Deutschland Regiment in July 1943. The collar Tresse and shoulder board style are particularly clear. Interestingly, for so late in the war, his tunic is the early pattern with dark green collar and scalloped pocket flaps (81/143/18A).

Obersturmführer Rudolf Lehmann wearing the early Germania Regiment collar patch, and armband. Lehmann later became Dietrich's right-hand man in the Leibstandarte and won the Knight's Cross in 1944 for his defence of the division's headquarters against a Soviet attack. He was the last commander of Das Reich *in Hungary and Austria (81/141/14).*

Obersturmbannführer Friedrich-Wilhelm Bock, an outstanding artillery officer, who won the Knight's Cross while CO of the 2nd Battalion of the SS-Polizei Artillery Regiment with Army Group North in 1943. He commanded Hohenstaufen *June-August 1944 during the Normandy fighting (81/141/6).*

Above left *Lacking cuff litle, but with the 'LAH' monogram on his shoulder boards, is a young Hauptsturmführer Joachim Peiper examining photographic contact strips in France, June 1940. All of the photographs in this book were reproduced directly from such strips, which accounts for their variable quality (81/141/15).*

Above right *An anxious Army infantryman waits while his papers are checked by an SS Feldgendarmerie NCO. Note helmet shield, gorget, sleeve eagle (compared to the Army breast eagle, also visible) and cuff title (81/143/28A).*

Above far right *This photogrpah, taken in June/July 1940, shows members of the* Deutschland *Regiment being decorated with Iron Crosses. The numeral '1' is just visible on the collar of the man on the left. The man to whose chest the ribbon is being pinned is a Rottenführer with double collar patch stripes and sleeve chevrons (75/118/34).*

Right *Dozing members of the SS-V Division in France, 1940, showing (left) the cap with soft grey peak and (right) the triangular eagle badge on the sidecap (81/146/1A).*

Left *Officers of the Polizei Division in Russia, winter 1941. They all wear riding breeches beneath tunics with pleated and scalloped pockets but, whereas the centre figure has a plain grey collar, the other two men have the earlier dark green version. Two styles of the field cap are visible, that on the left having the scalloped front and that on the right the original 'boat' shape (81/146/10A).*

Below left *Officers of the Leibstandarte discuss a mechanical breakdown. All wear the smart peaked cap, the Hauptscharführer in the centre without cords, of course; note also the NCO Tresse around his collar. The man on the left of the picture is an Untersturmführer, he on the right a Sturmbannführer. In the latter case, note also the dark green collar and the cuff title (81/141/9).*

Right *J. Hendrik ('Henk') Feldmeijer, Voorman (or commander) of the Nederlandsche-SS. This organisation derived from the prewar Mussert-Garde, the Dutch equivalent of the SS, and was later (1942) incorporated into the Germanische SS. Feldmeijer served with distinction in the Balkans with the Leibstandarte and in Russia with Wiking and in March 1943 was granted the regular SS rank of Standartenführer. He was killed during an air raid in February 1945 (81/141/2).*

Above left *Tropical kit: the lightweight yellow tunic with dark green (or black?) collar being worn by a* Totenkopf *Haupsturmführer in Russia, 1942. Note the divisional badge painted on the turret of the captured Soviet T-34 tank in the background. The chevron on his right arm denotes Party membership prior to January 30 1933 and was known as an Honour Stripe (75/118/9)*

Above *The same tunic being worn by a* Wiking *Division* Hauptscharführer. *Notice NCO Tresse around collar but complete lack of collar patches (75/118/23).*

Left *Contrary to popular belief, the dark green collar was still in use as late as 1944, as shown by this photograph of Knight's Cross holder Hauptscharführer Helmut Schreiber, from the* Wiking *Division, taken on January 10 of that year. Note his* Germania *cuff title and infantry assault and wound badges (81/141/25A)*

Hitler's Samurai

Above *Winter gear: a rough sheepskin jacket and woollen gloves, together with whitewashed helmet, being worn by a man of the* Langemarck *Division. Although no insignia are visible in this unpublished photograph, others in the same sequence clearly show to which unit he belongs (81/141/5).*

Above right *Winter gear: Joachim Peiper, on left of photo, wears a one-piece overall in grey with what appears to be a fur collar; while Fritz Witt, then commander of the 1st SS Panzergrenadier Regiment* Leibstandarte *Adolf Hitler, wears a sheepskin jerkin above his tunic, riding breeches and felt boots. Witt wears the Knight's Cross he won as CO of the* Deutsch-land *Regiment in 1940. He was killed by naval gunfire in Normandy in June 1944 and is buried at Champigny St André. Here, he wears the single oakleaf collar patches of a Standartenführer, and the picture is belived to have been taken in Kharkov during March 1943 (75/119/30).*

Right *Despite the snow, the Polizei cap badge is particularly clear in this picture taken in Finland/Lapland during the winter of 1941-42 (81/144/17A).*

Above left *The black Panzer uniform complete with beret being worn by a Rottenführer in the Balkans, 1941. The unit is probably* Das Reich. *The armoured car is an SdKfz 221. The character on the right, in light raincoat, is probably a local collaborator (75/120/18A).*

Above right *A* Das Reich *sentry in Russia during the summer of 1941. A white cloth cover prevents his helmet heating up too much in the sun. Behind him is a Staff pennant bearing the divisional device in its centre (75/120/26A).*

Opposite page

Top left *A Scharführer, commander of PzKpfw IV, wearing the mottle camouflage version of the Panzer jacket with two stripes on his left sleeve to denote rank. His cap piping is white apart from the waffenfarbe chevron, which appears to be Panzer pink (81/142/20).*

Top right *An Unterscharführer of a Norwegian volunteer unit showing one variant of the sleeve badge (81/148/12).*

Right *More details of SS Feldgendarmerie gear not shown in the earlier photograph are clear in this shot of an Unterscharführer wearing gorget and cuff title questioning Russian prisoners in the presence of a* Totenkopf *Sturmscharführer (centre) (81/142/5).*

Hitler's Samurai

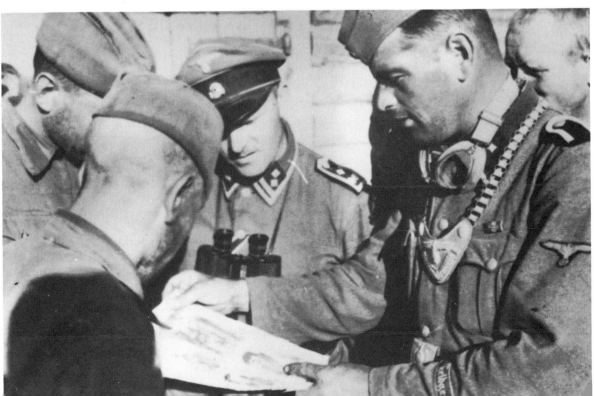

SS documentation and records

Whatever else it may have or may not have been, the Third Reich was the ultimate bureaucracy. *Everything* was documented, and lack of papers when stopped in the street would lead to an investigation under the most unpleasant circumstances unless you had a very good and valid reason or knew a high-ranking Party functionary who could vouch for you. Although SS uniform on its own was usually sufficient protection from interrogation, even members of the Schutzstaffeln would normally carry an impressive array of documents in their wallets to prove their identity and rank.

A fairly typical SS man was Georg Müller from Duisburg, some of whose documents are illustrated here. Müller joined the Nationalsozialistische Deutsche Arbeiterpartei early, in July 1926, and his first Ausweiskarte, or Party membership card, was a very basic product typed on red pasteboard. As the NSDAP grew, and its finances with it, new Party cards—properly printed—were issued, Müller receiving his in December 1931.

By this time he had also been issued—in August 1929—with his red Party Record Book, in which his personal details were recorded, such as (in this case) permission to attend a Nürnberg rally, and one in Brunswick, together with his SS promotions.

Müller was also an early entrant into the SS, number 4,700, which meant he also had to carry an SS Ausweiskarte bearing his photograph and signature. The illustrations show him in the black

Schutzstaffeln der N.S.D.A.P.

SS-Führer-
Ausweis Nr. 4 700

Pg. M ü l l e r , Georg

Mitglieds-Nr. 46 581

ift ϟϟ-Untersturmführer

in der Stammabt.West Bez.25

Eigenhändige Unterschrift

Befördert: 9.11.35. Ernannt: 1.4.36.

Berlin, den 26. März 193 6.

Der Reichsführer der Schutzstaffeln

i.V.

Ausweis nur gül... mit zeitlich richtiger Beglaubigungsmarke E

Allgemeine-SS uniform with the rank distinctions of an Untersturmführer in 1936.

When the war came, Müller did not join the SS-VT or Waffen-SS but instead was drafted (not an uncommon practice) into the Army. The idea of having an SS cadre in Wehrmacht units was to provide moral and political 'stiffening', but Müller also proved a competent soldier as well as an excellent prewar athlete and was twice awarded the Iron Cross, in Russia. He became an artillery officer and the last, and rarest, of the documents in his possession is his award, as an Oberleutnant in I/Feld Artillerie Regiment 1308 on April 20 1945, of the War Merit Cross 2nd Class with Swords.

Müller would also have had a Soldbuch recording his military career—decorations, transfers, periods of leave and suchlike; and a Wehrpass (military pass).

IM NAMEN DES FÜHRERS
VERLEIHE ICH
DEM
Oberleutnant
Georg Miller
I./F.A.Rgt.1308

DAS

KRIEGSVERDIENSTKREUZ
2. KLASSE
MIT SCHWERTERN

Div.Gef.Std., DEN 20.April 1945

(DIENSTSIEGEL)

Generalmajor u. Div. Kdr.
(DIENSTGRAD UND DIENSTSTELLUNG)

Facing page. Top *Georg Müller.* Bottom *Müller's SS Ausweiss.* This page. Above left *Two pages from his Party Record Book.* Above *Citation for the War Merit Cross.* Below left *Sports award in Gold.* Below and bottom *Müller's first and second NSDAP membership cards* (Christopher Ailsby Photographic Collection).

4. Weapons and equipment

There is a popular misconception that Waffen-SS units were better equipped than Army formations. In the case of the three premier divisions, Leibstandarte SS *Adolf Hitler, Das Reich* and *Totenkopf*, this was certainly true, but only from the beginning of 1943 when, after rest and refit, they returned to Russia as the SS Panzer Korps. As far as other units are concerned, almost the reverse, in fact applied.

At the beginning of the war only the Leibstandarte was motorised, the SS-VT and *Totenkopf* Standarten being infantry divisions employing predominantly horse-drawn transport. However, it must not be forgotten that this state of affairs was shared by the vast majority of the Army formations, only Guderian's six Panzer divisions (1-5 and 10) and the premier infantry division *Grossdeutschland* being fully motorised.

By the beginning of 1940, however, a further four Panzer divisions had been created (6-9) and the SS-VT and *Totenkopf* divisions were motorised; the Polizei formation was not, since it was not considered a front-line unit. Even at this stage, however, the Army refused to surrender any of its precious heavy artillery to the SS, and it required Hitler's personal intervention, in March 1940, before they received them: three heavy (15 cm) battalions were organised, one for each front-line division, plus a light (10.5 cm) battalion for the Leibstandarte. However, even these were captured Czech weapons, and it was not until 1942 that Albert Speer, with Hitler's support, agreed to allocate five to eight per cent of his factories' output to the Waffen-SS in return for the release of concentration camp inmates to work in those same factories.

It is obviously impossible in a book of this nature to list every piece of equipment used by the Waffen-SS, as this would run to several hundred items. What follows is, therefore, a précis of the most common weapons. Readers wishing a complete account are referred to the indispensable works *Small Arms, Artillery and Special Weapons of the Third Reich*, by Terry Gander and Peter Chamberlain (Macdonald and Jane's, 1978); and *Encyclopaedia of German Tanks of World War Two*, by Peter Chamberlain and Hilary Doyle (Arms and Armour Press, 1978); and other individual works on armoured cars, half-tracks and soft-skin transport vehicles available.

Infantry weapons

Pistols The German military machine preferred automatics to revolvers, the only examples of the latter category used being captured weapons of Russian, Polish, Greek, French and English origins. The standard sidearms were either the 9 mm P 08, popularly known as the 'Luger'; and the 9 mm P 38 designed by Walther but predominantly manufactured by Mauser. Both had eight-round magazines and a range of around 50 metres. Also widely used were the Walther PP and PPK, both of 7.65 mm calibre. These small, easily concealed weapons were especially popular with officers and tank crews. Of the 30-plus other pistols available, two found special favour with Waffen-SS troops. The first was the old Mauser C 96 in either 7.63 or 9 mm versions. This weapon,

Right *Good shot of a Czech 10 cm leFH 30(t)—to give it its German designation—being used by* Totenkopf *troops in 1940. This was but one of many captured weapons eagerly seized by the fledgling Waffen-SS in the face of Army recalcitrance over allocations (81/141/27).*

unmistakable by its ungainly 'broomstick' handle and wooden holster which doubled as a detachable shoulder stock, could take a 10- or 20-round magazine and was particularly favoured in anti-partisan duties. The other was the Polish ViS wz.35, a 9 mm automatic very similar in appearance to the American Colt .45. Apochryphal stories of a special 10.5 mm revolver issued to selected SS personnel are almost certainly figments of the imagination.

Rifles These fall into three categories: bolt-action, semi-automatic and automatic. In the first category the standard weapon was the Mauser Kar 98k, a derivative of the First World War Gew 98 with shortened barrel and other refinements. This weapon existed in many variations, being manufactured under the Nazi yoke in Czechoslovakia, Poland and Belgium in addition to Germany in 7.65, 7.9 and 7.92 mm calibre versions. It took a five-round magazine and could be fitted with a telescopic sight or a grenade launcher. Many other bolt-action rifles from occupied countries were also kept in production and service, although by and large they were not issued to front-line troops, and certainly not to the premier Waffen-SS divisions.

Surprisingly, the German Army which went to war in 1939 had no semi-automatic (self-loading) or automatic rifles, and it was only when the front-line troops began encountering Soviet Tokarev and Simonov weapons in 1941 that a crash programme was instigated to give them a comparable design. The first result was the totally inadequate Mauser Gew 41(M), which was rejected, and the barely acceptable Walther Gew 41(W). This 7.92 mm rifle took a ten-round magazine and could be fired at up to 40 rounds per minute. It was succeeded by the greatly improved Gew 43, which went into production towards the end of 1942. This weapon was not only cheaper to produce, relying largely on stamped instead of machined components, and having a laminated instead of a solid stock, but was also far more reliable in use. A version with a shortened barrel, known as the Kar 43, was introduced in 1944.

The first fully automatic rifle with selective fire characteristics was the MKb (Maschinenkarabiner) 42. The forerunner of all modern assault rifles, this existed in two forms, a Walther design which was abandoned following unsatisfactory troop trials in Russia, and a Schmeisser design manufactured by Haenel which was the direct ancestor of the MP 43 and StG 44. All these 7.92 mm weapons employed stamped rather than machined parts in their construction and took curved magazines holding 30 rounds. How the MP 40 sub-machine gun (see below) acquired the nickname 'Schmeisser' is unknown to me: it would have been much more appropriately applied to this range of weapons. Rate of fire in all cases was effectively 120 rounds per minute. It should be noted that the Waffen-SS *did* receive priority in deliveries of the MP 43.

Sub-machine-guns Probably the best-known German weapon of World War 2 is the MP 38, MP 38/40 and MP 40 series of revolutionary sub-machine-guns designed by Erma, of which well in excess of a million were produced. This weapon, with its lightweight folding stock and long 32-round magazine, was—and still is—a superb close-quarters design, far more accurate than the British Sten (or even the modern Sterling). It fires a 9 mm ball round at 390 metres per second. In addition to these SMGs, others available included the MP 28/II; the German copy of the Sten, but with a vertical magazine, known as the MP 3008; and the Czech ZK vz.383, a weapon with a far higher muzzle velocity (426 metres per second) which was kept in production exclusively for Waffen-SS use. Captured Russian weapons were also popular.

Machine-guns The standard, and by far the best and most widely used, machine-guns in the German inventory were the 7.92 mm MG 34 and its successor, the MG 42, which differed principally in its construction of largely pressed instead of machined steel components. Both were first class weapons with a very high cyclic rate of fire using 50-round belts of approximately 750 rounds per minute. Used as a section weapon on their bipods, they had an effective range of 5-600 metres, while as sustained fire heavy support weapons, on tripods, this was extended to some 2,000 metres. 50-round drum magazines

Right *A variety of weapons are visible in this posed shot of Leibstandarte troops in Kharkov, March 1943. The foreground machine-gun is an MG 42 on bipod mount in its LMG guise. The 'No 2' in the centre carries a spare 50-round belt of ammunition around his neck. The NCO on the right of the picture has an MP 40 sub-machine-gun slung from his right shoulder and a Stielgranate tucked in his belt (75/120/9A).*

Although of poor quality, this picture shows men of the Totenkopf *Division the moment after firing a captured Russian 8.2 cm mortar, which was given the designation GrW 274(r) in German service. It is impossible to tell whether this is the Mark 1 or 2 version (75/118/12).*

could also be clipped in place in either role for single-handed use. A combat advantage of the MG 42 was that its barrel could be changed very rapidly. Both single and twin mountings were available for anti-aircraft use.

No other type of machine-gun saw such widespread use as the MG 34/MG 42, although ex-Luftwaffe 13 mm and 15 mm weapons, the MG 131 and the MG 151/15, were adapted for ground use, and a wide variety of captured weapons from all sources were impressed into service, mainly by second-line, garrison and anti-aircraft units.

Mortars and grenades The standard German infantry mortar throughout the war was the 8 cm GrW 34 which could fire a 3.5 kg bomb up to 2,400 m. An attempt to produce a lighter 5 cm weapon, the leGrW 36, was not successful since it was too complicated and it was gradually withdrawn from 1941 onwards. To replace it at company level, the Waffen-SS adopted the short-barrelled version of the 8 cm weapon which had been designed for airborne

operations, designated kz 8 cm GrW 42. This only weighed 26.5 kg instead of the original weapon's 57 kg, but had less than half the range (1,100 m). At regimental level a 12 cm mortar, closely copied from the Soviet Polkovoy model, went into operation from late 1941. It had a two-wheeled carriage for towing and could hurl a 15.6 kg bomb to over 6,000 m. Many other captured mortars were also used, but rarely by SS units and then not as front line weapons.

The two normal types of hand grenade were the well-known Stielgranate, or stick grenade, and the Eiergranate, or egg grenade. The former contained a 0.62 kg TNT charge, the latter a 0.34 kg filling. For anti-tank use a most unusual grenade was developed, the Panzerwurfmine (L), which had a hollow charge warhead and folding canvas fins to keep it head-on to its target in flight.

Anti-tank weapons Anti-tank rifles were little used by the Waffen-SS as the French campaign had proved them practically worthless other than against the lightest tanks and armoured cars. After 1940 most were used in North Africa or issued to second-line units. This left the infantry very vulnerable to thickly armoured Soviet tanks until the introduction of the recoiless Panzerfaust in July and the 8.8 cm RPzP 43 'bazooka' later in the same year. The Panzerfaust comprised a launcher tube, open at both ends, containing a propellant charge, which varied in weight according to the model to give different ranges of 30 to 100 m. The warhead itself was a hollow charge projectile weighing 3 kg and capable of penetrating up to 200 mm of tank armour. The RPzB (Racketenpanzerbüchse) 43 was closely based on the American bazooka. An electrical trigger ignited an 8.8 cm rocket which could destroy most targets at up to 150 m range. However, it was dangerous to its user because of the long tail of rocket exhaust, and protective clothing, including a face mask with goggles, had to be worn until the introduction in 1944 of its successor, the RPzB 54, which had an integral shield. Later still, an improved propellant was devised which burnt entirely inside the launcher tube, eliminating the danger to the user and enabling the barrel itself to be shortened.

Hitler's Samurai

Flamethrowers These diabolical weapons comprise four basic components: a container of inflammable liquid, a container of compressed gas, a valve and a nozzle tube. Until the 1930s they had been bulky and heavy items requiring a three-man crew, but in 1935 a new model was introduced which was almost light enough for one man, even at 33.8 kg. This was followed by further improved models in 1940 and 1941, the final version using propellant cartridges instead of a gas tank because of problems encountered in the extreme cold of the Russian winter. The range of all flamethrowers was between 25 and 30 m, and up to ten one-second bursts could be fired. Some SS units also acquired the disposable flamethrower, a one-shot weapon originally designed to a Fallschirmjäger requirement, and known as the Einstossflammenwerfer 46.

Ordnance

Guns and howitzers These were normally classified as infantry guns, lighter weapons usually issued at regimental level; light field guns of up to 10.5 cm calibre; and medium and heavy artillery. However, there were certain weapons which did transcend the traditional groupings, such as the 15 cm sIG 33 (sIG = schweres Infanteriegeschütze), classed as an infantry gun. Like most German guns, this was available with different wheels according to whether it was to be horse-drawn or towed behind a vehicle. In different configurations it weighed 1,680-1,825 kg. A Rheinmetall design, it could fire up to three rounds a minute of high explosive, hollow charge or

smoke shells to a range of just under 5 km. The most common infantry gun, however, was the 7.5 cm leIG (leichtes Infanteriegeschütze) 18, a short barrelled weapon with a small splinter shield. Another Rheinmetall design, it weighed 400-570 kg and could fire a 6 kg shell up to 4½ km, with a rate of fire of 8-12 rpm. A lighter version with a different carriage, which could be broken down for mule transport, was introduced for mountain use under the designation 7.5 cm leichtes Gebirgsinfanteriegeschütz 18. A proposed air-portable version for paratroop use was discontinued in favour of recoilless guns after troop trials.

The standard light field gun for most of the war was the 7.5 cm leFK (leichte Feldkanone) 18, which combined a Rheinmetall barrel with a Krupp carriage. Weighing 1,120 kg without its limber, it could fire a 5.8 kg shell to 9½ km at 8-10 rpm. In the 10.5 cm bracket, the normal weapon was the leFH (leichtes Feldhaubitze) 18 and 18M, the latter being a modified version introduced in 1940 to give improved range. Both versions fired a 14.8 kg shell at 4-6 rpm, ranges being 10½ and 12½ km respectively. Both versions weighed 2,065 kg in action.

The most widely used heavy field howitzer (schweres Feldhaubitze) was the 15 cm sFH 18 which weighed 5,512 kg in action. It had a rate of fire of 4 rpm and could hurl a 43.5 kg shell to 13½

15 cm sFH 18 crewed by members of the SS-V in France, 1940 (81/141/28).

km. Also used was the 15 cm K (Kanone) 18, an unwieldy weapon whose barrel, carried on a special transporter, and carriage, had to be towed as separate loads. In action it weighed 12,460 kg and could fire a 43 kg shell to just under 25 km. The rate of fire was 2 rpm. Finally, the SS Panzer Divisions also used the heavy 17 cm Kanone 18, a large and modern Krupp design which entered service in 1941. Weighing 17,510 kg in action, it had a rate of fire of three shells every two minutes, the rounds being between 68 and 71 kg in weight (high explosive and armour piercing respectively). The gun's range was 28 km.

Anti-tank guns At the beginning of the war the basic anti-tank gun was the 3.7 cm Pak (Panzerabwehrkanone) 35/36, development of which had begun as early as 1928, by Rheinmetall. War experience rapidly showed that this weapon was, however, inadequate to the task, particularly when up against British Matilda tanks and, later, Soviet T-34s and KV-1s. In its original form it fired a 0.68 kg armour-piercing round with an effective range of 600 m, able to penetrate 46 mm of armour plate at

0° at this range. In 1940 a lighter (0.35 kg) round with 50 per cent greater muzzle velocity was introduced. The range was reduced to 400 m but penetration at this distance was 58 mm. Finally, from 1941, a hollow-charge grenade round came into service. The range was significantly reduced, to 200 m, but armour penetration rose drastically to no less than 180 mm at this range.

Entering service in April 1940, although it is my belief that Waffen-SS formations did not receive it until the end of the year, was the 5 cm Pak 38. Like all German (and unlike British) anti-tank weapons, this could fire high explosive as well as solid armour piercing shot. The AP round weighed 0.92 kg and had a useful range of well over 1,000 m, being able to penetrate 84 mm of armour at that range or 120 mm at half that.

Moving up the scale, the 7.5 cm Pak 40 did not enter service until late in 1941 but proved an outstanding weapon. Two ammunition rounds were available, the earlier weighing 6.8 kg and having a range of up to 2,000 m, at which it could penetrate

98 mm of armour plate (121 mm at 1,000 m, 135 mm at 500 m); and the later round weighing 3.2 kg which had a range of up to 2,500 m and was able to penetrate 98 mm at 2,000 m, 133 mm at 1,000 m and 154 mm at 500 m.

Most famous of all German guns was the dreaded '88'. Originally designed as an anti-aircraft weapon by Krupp, it first saw action with the Condor Legion in Spain and later with all branches of the German armed forces, as a dual-purpose anti-aircraft/anti-tank gun. The first version to go into service was the Flak (Flugabwehrkanone) 18. This was a very clever design, the gun being mounted on a central 'leg' with two folding outriggers which were laid flat when the gun was removed from its two wheeled trailers to provide a stable cruciform firing platform. Unlimbered for action in this way, the Flak 18 weighed 5,150 kg. However, it was soon discovered that the barrel life was too short so a modified version, with special 'disposable' barrel liners, known as the Flak 36, was introduced. The definitive version, the Flak 37, with improved

sighting and ranging gear, came into service a year later (1937). All three variants, however, served side by side throughout the war, although the Flak 36 was the most common in the field, the 18 gradually being relegated to second-line duties and the 37 to anti-aircraft defence for the vital Ruhr and other industrial centres.

The Flak 36 (which was later mounted in the Tiger tank with the designation KwK 36) fired a 9.5-10.2 kg round in the anti-tank role at 770-810 m/sec muzzle velocity. It had an effective range of up to 2,500 m but was still deadly at well beyond that. Armour penetration at 2,000, 1,000 and 500 mm respectively was 72-88 mm, 87-106 mm and 93-117 mm, depending on the ammunition used. Later, a lighter charge (7.3 kg) with a higher muzzle velocity (930 m/sec) was introduced which could penetrate 110, 138 and 156 mm respectively at the above ranges.

Although it was a superb weapon, the Flak 36 suffered from several defects in the anti-tank role, one of the worst being its height off the ground which made it a vulnerable target for enemy fire. Moreover, the increasing armour thickness of tanks meant that something even better was required and, by the end of 1941, Krupp had evolved the more powerful Flak 41—which did not, however, enter service until 1943 due to 'teething troubles'. With a lower carriage and a longer barrel (L/71 instead of L/56) giving a higher muzzle velocity of 980 m/sec, this weapon had an armour-piercing capability of 132, 165 and 185 mm respectively at 2,000, 1,000 and 500 m.

However, Krupp then went on to produce the best German anti-tank gun of all, the Pak 43, with even greater muzzle velocity (1,130 m/sec) giving armour penetration of 153, 193 and 217 mm respectively at the above ranges. A variant, produced because manufacture of the carriage could not keep pace with that of the barrels, was the Pak 43/41, a Pak 43 barrel mounted on a leFH 18 *(qv)* carriage.

In 1944 the largest of the anti-tank guns began entering service, the 12.8 cm Pak 44. Similar in appearance to the Pak 43, although larger and heavier, it fired a 28 kg projectile at 950 m/sec but

Autumn 1941. A 15 cm sFH 18 of the Totenkopf *Division is towed past a Flak 36 deployed in the anti-tank role* (81/143/30A).

was actually *less* effective than the lighter Pak 43, with armour-piercing ability of 148, 167 and 178 mm at the usual ranges.

Side by side with the above standard developments the German arms industry also produced both tapered-bore and recoilless anti-tank guns. A tapered bore gun 'squeezes' the shot, which itself is usually of tungsten to give the greatest weight for size, enhancing the muzzle velocity and giving a relatively small calibre weapon a lethal effectiveness. The smallest of these was the Gehrlich 2.8 cm sPzB 41 which only fired a shot weighing 0.12 kg but which had a muzzle velocity of 1,400 m/sec. The effective range was limited to no more than 500 mm, at which it could penetrate 40 mm of armour. The gun gradually fell into disuse as it was ineffective against most Soviet tanks from 1942 onwards, and shortage of tungsten meant little ammunition could be manufactured. The same fate befell the 4.2 cm Pak 41 and 7.5 cm Pak 41.

Recoilless weapons were designed for airborne and mountain use, and some found their way to the SS Fallschirm- and Gebirgsjäger formations. Very few of any type were manufactured, production of all ceasing in 1944, and the only one specifically designed for anti-tank use (although they all had a dual role) was the 7.5 cm RiK 43 which could penetrate 120 mm of armour plate at 200 m. As with all recoilless weapons, the main disadvantage was the severe backlash which gave away its position to the enemy the moment it fired.

Anti-aircraft guns Smallest of the German anti-aircraft guns was the 20 mm Flak 30 and its derivative, the Flak 38. Designed for use against low-flying ground attack aircraft (or, in its naval guise, for point defence), it took a 20-round magazine giving a practical rate of fire of 120 rpm at targets up to some 2,000 m. From 1940, a new carriage was designed mounting four Flak 38s co-axially. This was a deadly weapon against aircraft and lightly armoured vehicles, frequently being deployed in the ground role.

The next calibre was the 3.7 cm Flak 36 and Flak 37, which fired six-round clips giving a rate of fire of 80-100 rpm. Although its range was no greater than that of the Flak 38, its heavier round (0.68 kg instead of 0.30 kg) gave it a heavier punch, and it could, of course, fire the same ammunition as the Pak 35/36, giving it a rapid fire anti-tank capability.

From late 1943 onwards an improved version, the Flak 43, entered service. This had eight-round clips, improving the rate of fire to 150 rpm, and the range was more than doubled to 4,200 m. A twin mounting, with the barrels horizontally superimposed, made this weapon even more effective.

Both 20 mm and 3.7 cm anti-aircraft guns were mounted on self-propelled carriages (see below).

In the medium range, German forces used small numbers of 5 cm anti-aircraft weapons, none of which were very satisfactory and are therefore unlikely to have been issued to SS formations.

The best-known of the German anti-aircraft weapons was the 8.8 cm Flak 18, 36 and 37 described above, plus the Flak 41. In the anti-aircraft role, the 18/36/37 had a rate of fire of 15-20 rpm and a ceiling of 10,600 m; the Flak 41 a rate of 20-25 rpm and a ceiling of 14,700 m.

Finally, German field forces also used substantial numbers of the 10.5 cm Flak 38 and Flak 39, although these were never as numerous as the '88 variants (at the peak period, August 1944, there were 10,704 Flak 18s, 36s and 37s in service compared with 1,969 Flak 38s and 39s). These guns fired 12-15 15 kg rounds per minute to a ceiling of 12,800 m.

Other German anti-aircraft guns, from 12.8 cm calibre upwards, were used in static fixed emplacements, not in the field.

Foreign weapons The Germans captured huge stocks of weapons in all the occupied countries, as well as manufacturing plants, particularly in Belgium and Czechoslovakia. All of these were pressed into service, mostly with second-line formations and in fortifications (although *Prinz Eugen*, uniquely, used Czech weapons almost exclusively), which are far too numerous to list here. Of special significance, and worthy of a brief note, is the Russian 7.62 cm Pak 36(r), an excellent dual-purpose anti-tank/field gun comparable to the Pak 40, which was used in substantial numbers by Army and Waffen-SS units.

Armoured vehicles

Tanks By the time the Waffen-SS started to receive tanks, for the Russian invasion, the early PzKpfw Is and IIs were obsolete and the PzKpfw III (except for the Ausf L and M) obsolescent. The main equipment was therefore the PzKpfw IV Ausf F2 and G, armed with 7.5 cm KwK40 L/48 guns, and their successors, the Ausf H (the most numerous variant) and J. These differed mainly in detail—transmission, muzzle brake, vision ports and armour. Almost all vehicles were fitted or retrofitted with spaced armour—schürzen—as protection against hollow-charge weapons. The basic vehicle weighed 23-25 tons and had eight road wheels and four return rollers. It was powered by a Maybach engine through a gearbox giving six forward and one reverse gears and a speed of 38 km/h. The range was normally 200-220 km, although in the Ausf J this increased to 320 since the powered turret traverse mechanism was removed to give extra space for fuel. Armour thickness (Ausf H) was 50-80 mm at the front, 30 mm at the sides, 20-30 mm at the rear and 10-15 mm top and bottom. A crew of five was carried—commander, driver, co-driver/hull machine-gunner, gunner and loader.

The Waffen-SS was also equipped with the heavy PzKpfw VI Tiger, which entered service earlier than the Mark V Panther. The Tiger was a massive 57-ton vehicle mounting the 8.8 cm KwK36 L/56 gun plus two machine-guns. It had eight sets of inter-leaved road wheels with torsion bar suspension and two different sets of tracks could be fitted—narrow for road use and for when being transported by rail, and wide for cross-country duties. It was powered by a Maybach engine through a gearbox giving eight forward and four reverse gears and a speed of 38 km/h. The range was 140 km. The Tiger was very heavily armoured: 100-110 mm front, 60-80 mm sides, 80 mm rear and 25 mm top and bottom. It also had a crew of five.

The famous PzKpfw V Panther, which did not enter production until January 1943, was a 43-ton vehicle featuring well-sloped armour copied from the Russian T-34 in contrast to the box-shape of earlier German tanks. It had eight pairs of road wheels and torsion bar suspension. It was produced in three versions, all powered by the same Maybach engine with a seven forward and one reverse gearbox giving

PzKpfw IVF2 of an unidentified Waffen-SS unit in Russia, 1943 (81/142/21).

a speed of 46 km/h. All three versions had the same main armament of a 7.5 cm KwK42 L/70 high-velocity gun. The earliest mark, the Ausf D, did not have a hull machine-gun. One was introduced on the second mark, the Ausf A, initially through a 'letter box' opening, although this was replaced during the production run, and on the final mark, the Ausf G, by a ball mounting. The Panther was not as heavily armoured as the Tiger, but the slope of its armour effectively compensated for this: 60-100 mm front, 40-45 mm sides and rear, 16-30 mm top and bottom. As with other German tanks, a crew of five was carried. By the end of the war, Panthers formed over half the strength of the Panzer divisions.

The final German tank issued to the Waffen-SS was the PzKpfw VIB Tiger II or 'King Tiger'. This massive 68-ton vehicle was ludicrously underpowered having the same engine as in the Panther. In appearance it looked more like a scaled-up Panther than a Tiger, though having the same sloped armour. It mounted the long-barreled 8.8 cm KwK 43 L/71 gun plus hull and co-axial turret machine-guns. Two turrets were in fact issued, one designed by Porsche of which only 50 were produced, and that designed by Henschel which was fitted to the remaining 439 vehicles. The Tiger II had eight forward and four reverse gears and a speed of 35 km/h. Its frontal armour was exceptionally thick, 60-180 mm; sides and rear were 80 mm and top and bottom 40 mm. It also had a crew of five.

Self-propelled guns The German armed forces made great use of self-propelled guns of all types, some designed to extend the useful life of obsolete tank hulls and others custom-designed for specific purposes. They broadly fall into the following categories: assault guns, self-propelled artillery pieces, self-propelled anti-aircraft vehicles and tank hunter-killers. The earliest assault gun was the StuG III, based on the PzKpfw III chassis. These vehicles were initially equipped with the short 7.5 cm StuK37 L/24 and later with the long StuK40 L/43 or L/48 or the 10.5 cm StuH42 L/28 howitzer.

The StuG IV combined a PzKpfw IV chassis with the same superstructure as on the StuG III and had

Left A Grille self-propelled gun—a marriage between the 15 cm sIG gun and a PzKpfw 38(t) chassis (81/144/15A). Inset A Demag light half-track (SdKfz 10) towing a 3.7 cm Pak 35/36 in France, 1940 (81/141/26).

the 7.5 cm StuK40 L/48 fitted as standard. Later, a revised superstructure featuring sloped armour was designed to go around the 7.5 cm PaK39 L/48; this vehicle became known as the Jagdpanzer IV. Still later versions mounted the PaK42 L/70 and had other detail changes, notably to the rubber-rimmed wheels which could not carry the increased frontal weight and were therefore replaced by steel-rimmed versions. Other self-propelled weapons on the PzKpfw IV chassis which were used by SS divisions included the Möbelwagen 3.7 cm, Wirbelwind quad 20 mm and Ostwind 3.7 cm anti-aircraft vehicles. In addition, a lengthened PzKpfw IV chassis, utilising PzKpfw III components, formed the basis for the very successful Hummel 15 cm self-propelled howitzer and the 8.8 cm Pak 43 L/71-armed Hornisse or Nashorn tank hunter-killer.

Other self-propelled vehicles known to have been used by Waffen-SS formations include the 7.5 cm PaK40/3 auf PzKpfw 38(t) Ausf H which was issued to the Leibstandarte in December 1942; and the similar Marder III, both based on the Czech PzKpfw 38(t) tank chassis; plus the 10.5 cm howitzer-armed Wespe, which was based on the PzKpfw II chassis and entered service early in 1943. The only SS unit believed to have used the excellent Jagdpanther was *Hohenstaufen*, and they only had ten.

Other vehicles

There are far too many of these to enumerate here since the Waffen-SS used the whole range of soft-skin and half-tracked vehicles available to the Army, from BMW, Zundapp and other motor cycles upwards. These included the ubiquitous Kubelwagen, the Opel Blitz and a wide variety of other four-, six- and eight-wheeled trucks, SdKfz 250 and 251 armoured half-tracks, and four-, six- and eight-wheeled armoured cars.

Camouflage and markings

Broadly speaking, SS practice duplicated that of the Army. Pre-war, vehicles and artillery pieces were either dark grey in colour or else mottled in dark yellow, green and brown. During the Polish, 1940 and Balkan campaigns, all vehicles seem to have been dark grey. Following the invasion of Russia, mottled patterns began to reappear and, from 1942, most armoured vehicles seem to have left the factories in plain yellow finish, cans of green, brown

and grey paint being issued for units to apply as they best thought fit in the field. This resulted in a bewildering array of mottles, stripes and stipples, at least some of which were in direct imitation of the camouflage patterns on Waffen-SS combat smocks. Whitewash was almost universally used during the Russian winters, since it could be easily removed when the spring thaw arrived, but this weathered very quickly, leading to a grubby, patchy effect.

Little standardisation was ever reached in the application of insignia either. Even the national cross, which appeared in a wide variety of styles—as a black cross, with or without a white outline, as a white or black outline only, etc—was not always applied. Similarly, the three-digit vehicle numbering system was never adhered to strictly: this was supposed to denote, in the order 123, a vehicle's company, platoon and individual number—thus the above example would be the third vehicle of the 2nd Platoon of the 1st Company within a battalion or regiment. These numbers were also painted in a variety of ways and colours, although black or red, in solid or outline form, with or without a white border, and white outline styles seem to have been the most common. Tactical insignia, usually very small and painted in white or yellow, were stylised symbols denoting a vehicle's function; several examples can be seen in the photographs. They were more commonly applied to soft-skin and half-track vehicles than to tanks or self-propelled guns, whose role was pretty obvious anyway!

Divisional insignia were widely applied during the early war years but their use gradually dropped away and it is rare to see any such devices in late war photographs, the Leibstandarte and *Hitler Jugend* divisions being exceptions to the general rule. Panther tanks in particular very rarely carried any divisional markings. The accompanying drawings show the basic Waffen-SS divisional markings, which were normally painted in white (though sometimes in yellow, grey or black) on hull fronts and rears.

Other vehicle markings included Staff pennants, aerial recognition flags, individual slogans, nicknames and other devices applied by a vehicle's crew, and special tactical insignia for specific operations such as one-, two- and three-bar markings applied to Leibstandarte, *Das Reich* and *Totenkopf* tanks for the Kursk operation.

Left *Waffen-SS formation signs.* 1 *1st SS Panzer Division Leibstandarte* Adolf Hitler, *also worn within a shield and with two oakleaves by Korps vehicles.* 2 *2nd SS Panzer Division* Das Reich. 3 *Das Reich* Kursk marking. 4 *3rd SS Panzer Division* Totenkopf. 5 *4th SS Polizei Panzergrenadier Division.* 6 *Polizei Division variant.* 7 *5th SS Panzer Division* Wiking. 8 *6th SS Gebirgs Division* Nord. 9 *Nord Division variant.* 10 *7th SS Freiwilligen Gebirgs Division* Prinz Eugen. 11 *8th SS Kavallerie Division* Florian Geyer. 12 *9th SS Panzer Division* Hohenstaufen. 13 *Hohenstaufen Division variant, in red, used after Arnhem.* 14 *10th SS Panzer Division* Frundsberg. 15 *Frundsberg Division variant, white on yellow rhomboid.* 16 *11th SS Freiwilligen Panzergrenadier Division* Nordland. 17 *Nordland Division variant.* 18 *12th SS Panzer Division* Hitlerjugend. 19 *13th Waffen Gebirgs Division der SS* Handschar. 20 *Handschar Division variant.* 21 *14th Waffen Grenadier Division der SS.* 22 *15th Waffen Grenadier Division der SS.* 23 *15th Division variant.* 24 *16th SS Panzergrenadier Division* Reichsführer-SS. 25 *17th SS Panzergrenadier Division* Götz von Berlichingen. 26 *18th SS Freiwilligen Panzergrenadier Division* Horst Wessel. 27 *Horst Wessel Division variant.* 28 *Unconfirmed device for 19th Waffen Grenadier Division der SS; number 23 may have been used instead.* 29 *Possible 19th Division variant.* 30 *20th Waffen Grenadier Division der SS.* 31 *21st Waffen Gebirgs Division der SS* Skanderberg. 32 *22nd Freiwilligen Kavallerie Division der SS* Maria Theresia. 33 *23rd Waffen Gebirgs Division der SS* Kama. 34 *23rd Freiwilligen Panzergrenadier Division* Niederland/Nederland. 35 *24th Waffen Gebirgs Division der SS* Karstjäger. 36 *25th Waffen Grenadier Division der SS* Hunyadi. 37 *26th Waffen Grenadier Division der SS.* 38 *27th SS Freiwilligen Grenadier Division* Langemarck. 39 *28th SS Freiwilligen (Panzer) Division* Wallonien. 40 *Wallonien Division variant.* 41 *29th Waffen Grenadier Division der* SS (Russische Nr 1). 42 *29th Waffen Grenadier Division der* SS (Italienische Nr 1). 43 *30th Waffen Grenadier Division der SS.* 44 *31st SS Freiwilligen (Panzer) Grenadier Division* Böhmen-Mähren. 45 *Böhmen-Mähren Division variant.* 46 *32nd Freiwilligen/Panzer Grenadier Division* 30 Januar. 47 *33rd Waffen Kavallerie Division der SS (unconfirmed).* 48 *33rd Waffen Grenadier Division* Charlemagne. 49 *34th SS Freiwilligen Grenadier Division* Landstorm Nederland *(also displayed vertically).* 50 *35th SS Polizei Grenadier Division.* 51 *36th Waffen Grenadier Division der SS.* 52 *37th SS Freiwilligen Kavallerie Division* Lützow. 53 *38th SS Grenadier Division* Nibelungen. *(Drawings by John Major, reproduced from* World War 2 Military Vehicle Markings, *by Terence Wise, courtesy of the publishers, Patrick Stephens Limited.)*

Left *NCO of the* Totenkopf *Division in Russia in 1941. A Luger holster hangs from his left hip, a map case on the right. Strapped across his back is an MP 28/II, an obsolescent weapon derived from Schmeisser's original 1917 design for the first real sub-machine-gun. Although the Waffen-SS suffered through being allocated generally inferior equipment until 1942 at least, this weapon was usually only issued to garrison, second-line and police troops. This man may well therefore belong to one of the Einsatz-gruppen (81/143/32A).*

Below left *The Mauser 9 mm P 38 wielded by a soldier of the Leibstandarte in Kharkov, March 1943. Note his parka (75/119/26).*

Right *SS grenadiers with a flamethrower (94/437/32A).*

Above *SS-V troops in action with a 3.7 cm Pak 35/36 in France, 1940 (81/146/14A).*
Below *Rare picture on several accounts. The weapon is a 2.8 cm sPzB 41 but it has the light airborne carriage (Feldlafette 41) and a secondary splinter shield. Unusual to say the least! The crew is definitely SS, however, and the occasion the winter of 1942-3 (81/144/3A).*
Right *Men of an SS unit setting up a 15 cm NbW 41 in Russia, 1943 (81/144/11A).*

Hitler's Samurai

Above *A captured weapon, the French 4.7 cm Puteaux anti-tank gun (given the German designation Pak 181/183(f), being used for training purposes by* Totenkopf *personnel (18/141/33).*

Below *A 10.5 cm leFH 18 being loaded on to a landing barge in anticipation of the planned invasion of England in 1940 by members of the SS-V (81/146/16A).*

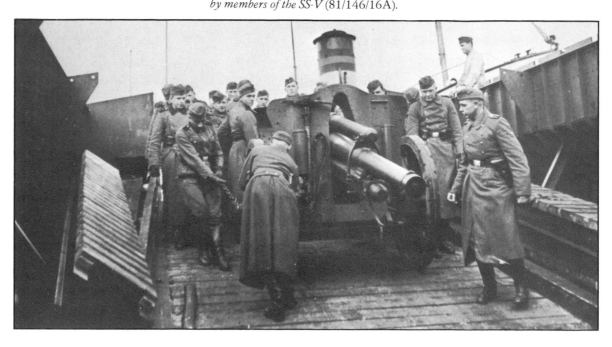

Hitler's Samurai

Above Men of the Wiking *Division operating a 15 cm sIG 33 in Russia, summer 1942* (81/144/18).

Below 8.8 cm Flak 36 at maximum recoil after firing. The gun is here apparently being used in the artillery support role (81/144/12A).

A Tiger 1 of the Leibstandarte showing clearly the Korps
badge—crossed keys within a shield, above two oak leaves
(299/1805/2).

This photograph *PzKpfw IVF2s of the* Totenkopf *Division with the special Kursk marking clearly visible on the foreground vehicle (81/144/5A).*

Below *PzKpfw VG Panther of the* Wiking *Division, May 1944 (81/144/29A).*

Hitler's Samurai

This photograph *StuG IIIG of an SS assault gun unit at the time of the battle of Kursk (81/142/22).*

Below *A Schwerer Panzerspähwagen (heavy armoured car) SdKfz 232 (Funk) drives past a car on whose mudguard the death's head device of a* Totenkopf *regiment is clearly visible, France 1940 (81/142/7).*

5. The Waffen-SS at war

One of the more frequent complaints levelled against the Waffen-SS is that its troops suffered unnecessarily high casualties in battle due to excess zeal, aggressiveness and poor leadership. Despite HIAG's protestations to the contrary, in 1939-40 there was a considerable element of truth in these accusations. Thereafter, however, any undue casualties suffered by the Waffen-SS can simply be attributed to the fact that any élite group which is kept semi-permanently in the front line is bound to suffer them. Moreover, hitting the enemy hard and fast, as the Army's own Panzer commanders found, minimises casualties, rather than the other way round; and the Waffen-SS's leadership was so 'poor' that its units were in constant demand, particularly in Russia, to act as mobile fire brigades wherever the fighting was expected to be the most fierce. In fact, it almost seems in some instances as though the Army deliberately sacrificed Waffen-SS units rather than accept casualties amongst its own men. Statistics are, unfortunately, elusive. The Waffen-SS lost some 253,000 men killed or missing, presumed dead, during the course of the Second World War—just over a quarter of its eventual total strength. The Army lost approximately 3,280,000: over a third of its strength. Perhaps, then, the truth is rather the reverse of that usually stated and SS 'aggressiveness' in the long run actually *saved* lives.

Another factor which may have contributed to the heavy casualties in 1939 is the fact that Waffen-SS units had little independent freedom of action, but were split up amongst various Army formations to sink or swim. *Deutschland*, together with the recently formed SS artillery regiment and reconnaissance Sturmbann, was brigaded with the 7th and 8th Panzer Regiments in Kempf's battlegroup for the invasion of Poland and participated in the fierce fighting for Brest-Litovsk. *Germania* remained in reserve with the 14th Army but saw some fighting during the occupation of the Lemberg area. The Leibstandarte had a rough time of it, attached to the 17th Infantry Division in the south. Because it was a motorised formation, it was used for reconnaissance and mobile flank defence, and saw heavy fighting around Pabianice in particular. The Leibstandarte was then re-allocated to 4th Panzer Division and fought its way through Lodz to the outskirts of Warsaw, then back westwards to help in the first major German encirclement manoeuvre of the war, in the bend of the River Bzura. The campaign culminated for the SS in the capture of the fortress of Modlin, which guarded the northern approach to Warsaw itself. The more recently formed *Der Führer* Regiment did not take part in this campaign since it was still not fully trained. One Totenkopf Sturmbann, *Götze*, did, however, acting as a small-scale forerunner of the later Einsatzgruppen in the Danzig area.

The Polish campaign, as discussed in chapter 2, had the beneficial effect of persuading Hitler to allow an expansion of the armed SS into what effectively became three divisions by May 1940: *Deutschland*, *Germania* and *Der Führer* in the SS-V* Division,

*The title SS-VT had been dropped in 1939.

Left *Near Bethune, May 24/25 1940. Men of the* Totenkopf *Division advance under fire. The armoured car is a captured Panhard with hastily applied German markings* (81/142/11).

the *Totenkopf* Standarten, and the reinforced Leibstandarte *Adolf Hitler* Brigade. The new Polizei Division which was in the process of being formed did not take an active part in the 1940 campaigns, being assigned a static watching role opposite part of the Maginot Line.

Stein* makes an interesting observation about relations between the Army and the SS at this time which is well worth quoting in full. The *Totenkopf* Division was assigned to Max Weichs' 2nd Army for the invasion of the west. On April 4 1940 he paid his first visit to Eicke's pride and joy.

'In their opening conversation with Eicke, Weichs and his staff revealed their ignorance about the new division that had been added to their command. They were under the impression that the *Totenkopf* Division was "organised and equipped like a Czech foot division"†, and were very much surprised to discover it was really a modern, motorised infantry division. At a time when only seven of the German Army's 139 infantry divisions were motorised this was indeed a command to be proud of. And when Eicke added the information that a heavy artillery section was being organised for the division, Weichs' professional interest was aroused and his coolness began to dissipate. Weichs' inspection of the troops left him visibly impressed, and he completed his visit in a frame of mind far different from that in which he had arrived.'

The SS divisions assembled for the invasion of France and the Low Countries were disposed as follows: the Leibstandarte and the *Der Führer* Regiment poised on the Dutch border ready to race ahead and link up with the Fallschirmjäger who had been entrusted with the vital task of capturing key bridges and fortifications‡, the remainder of the SS-V Division alongside the 9th Panzer Division; and *Totenkopf* in reserve

At dawn on May 10 the Leibstandarte overpowered the Dutch border guards facing them and raced towards its first objective, the twin bridges at Zwolle, a hundred kilometres away. Stopping for nothing, the motorised unit reached its target by midday, an achievement which is not diminished by the fact that

the Dutch had succeeded in demolishing the bridges. It found a crossing over the River Ijssel (Yssel) further south and pushed on another 70 kilometres, Obsrsturmführer Kraas winning the first Iron Cross First Class of the campaign in the process. Meanwhile, *Der Führer* spearheaded the advance of the 227th Infantry Division near Arnhem, immediately becoming involved in heavy fighting for the Grebbe Line; while 9th Panzer Division and the remainder of the SS-V crossed the Maas and headed towards Moerdijk, where paratroops had landed to seize another important bridge. The Leibstandarte, having achieved its own initial objectives, was switched to the south to join them.

9th Panzer and the SS-V moved together to halt a French thrust up through Belgium while the Leibstandarte moved on to relieve the Fallschirmjäger at Moerdijk and break through towards Rotterdam. The French were forced back and 9th Panzer's tanks also headed towards the city, leaving the SS-V to mop up. Following the infamous bombing of Rotterdam, the city surrendered and the Leibstandarte moved in before pressing on to The Hague. By the time they reached this objective the Dutch had surrendered so, after a victory march in Amsterdam, the Leibstandarte switched to the south once more and the main enemy, France. The Dutch naval garrisons in Zeeland had not capitulated, however, and these became the *Deutschland* Regiment's next task. With heavy air support, the SS troops won through to the coast, Dutch survivors being evacuated by sea.

Meanwhile, Eicke's *Totenkopf* Division had been brought out of reserve and attached to Rommel's 7th Panzer Division. After mopping-up operations in the Cambrai area, the two divisions received a check to both their headlong advance and their pride when they were held up and roughly mauled by a British counter-attack at Arras. The lumbering Matilda tanks had armour which was impervious to the 3.7 cm Pak 35/36 and it was only Rommel's deployment of a line of his 8.8 cm anti-aircraft guns in an anti-tank role which finally halted the British.

At this point the German advance had opened a huge salient between the bulk of the French Army to the south and the British and Belgian troops to the east of Dunkirk. It was therefore decided to pinch off the northern threat to the advance. Both the SS-V and the Leibstandarte distinguished themselves, Felix

---

*The Waffen-SS: Hitler's élite guard at war 1939-1945—see bibliography.
†As, indeed, *was* the embryo Polizei Division at this stage.
‡See *Fallschirmjäger*, by Bruce Quarrie, (Osprey Men-At-Arms series, 1983).

A column of Leibstandarte vehicles during the victorious advance. Note the key symbol which became the Leibstandarte's trade mark: it was chosen in honour of the unit's commander, 'Sepp' Dietrich, 'dietrich' being the German word for 'skeleton key' (81/141/12).

Steiner's *Deutschland* Regiment forcing a crossing of the River Lys and the Leibstandarte the Aa Canal. Men of Eicke's *Totenkopf* Division were, however, responsible for the first recorded major atrocity of the war, when the 2nd Company of the *Brandenburg* Regiment, under Obersturmführer Fritz Knochlein, was responsible for cold-bloodedly machine-gunning a hundred prisoners of war from the 2nd Royal Norfolks. Unknown to them, two survivors lay buried beneath the bodies. They later crawled away and, after being treated for their wounds by French civilians, were found and taken prisoner by a German Army unit. They were hospitalised and eventually repatriated at the end of the war, when it took them some time to overcome official disbelief of their account. It had been hushed up internally in the *Totenkopf* Division, despite strenuous attempts by Gruppenführer Hans Jüttner (in the Führungshauptamt) to bring the culprits to justice, supported by Gunther d'Alquen (later head of the Waffen-SS war correspondent service), who had seen the bodies. However, Knochlein was finally brought to justice and hanged in 1948.

The SS units continued to assist the Army in compressing the Allied salient around Dunkirk, an operation in which 'Sepp' Dietrich, commander of the Leibstandarte, nearly lost his life when his staff car was shot up and he and his driver had to shelter for several hours in a ditch while a battle raged above their heads*. However, the SS divisions were all withdrawn before the trapped British Expeditionary Force was either rescued by sea or captured, as their motorised abilities were now needed for the major advance into France. Before tackling this task, however, replacement troops from the training schools in Germany were rushed to join them, because losses had been grievous: 2,020 in the SS-V, 1,140 in Totenkopf and 270 in the Leibstandarte. (After the

*It was during the subsequent fighting around Wormhoudt that men of the Leibstandarte were also responsible for the shooting of some 80 British prisoners of war, on May 28, a fact which Lucas and Cooper, in *Hitler's Élite: Leibstandarte SS*, do not even mention.

campaign, the Waffen-SS was to incur severe criticism from the Army for the level of their casualties, but these are quite understandable when you consider both the aggressive manner in which they went into action against some of the most fiercely defended objectives, and the fact that, being motorised, they were constantly in the spearhead of the advance, alongside the Panzer Divisions.)

The SS-V and the Leibstandarte were both attached to von Kleist's Panzergruppe, the *Totenkopf* initially being held in reserve again. Attacking across the River Somme on June 6, the Panzergruppe initially made good progress, but French resistance grew stronger the closer the Germans approached to the north of Paris, and the attack was called off. Moved east, to the vicinity of Laon, the Leibstandarte went straight back into action with Guderian's Panzergruppe, heading south through Chateau-Thierry; the remainder of von Kleist's forces enjoyed a brief

three-day rest before following in their wake, *Toten-kopf* also being brought out of reserve to assist.

This time there was no stopping the Panzer and motorised SS divisions. Sweeping south through central France, they delayed for nothing; Paris was declared an open city on June 10 and the French Army appeared in imminent danger of complete collapse. Led by Dietrich, the Leibstandarte were to the fore in practically every encounter. But, apart from isolated strongpoints of French resistance, the advance encountered little resistance and rapidly turned into a headlong pursuit, the SS-V being in Dijon on June 16 and Lyons four days later, after beating off a French counter-attack on the 17th. The Leibstandarte was still to the fore, however, effecting a link-up with other German troops at Vichy and penetrating as far south as St Etienne. But, by this time, the French government had collapsed and Marshal Pétain was frantically discussing an armistice. However, it is worth mentioning that the Polizei Division had its first taste of blood in these final days of the campaign, assisting in the attack across the River Aisne and the Ardennes Canal on June 9-10 and then fighting its way through a French rearguard in the Argonne Forest.

For their achievements during these campaigns, the Waffen-SS formations were publicly praised by Hitler on July 19 in a speech to the Reichstag; and Dietrich, Steiner and Georg Keppler (commander of the *Der Führer* Regiment), were all awarded the Knight's Cross. All three had clearly demonstrated

what the Waffen-SS could accomplish when well led. Eicke and Pfeffer-Wildenbruch had, however, shown the opposite side of the coin, in that, although their troops had achieved all that was asked of them, inadequate training and leadership produced a far higher proportional casualty rate.

As discussed in chapter 2, the success of the campaigns in the west and preparations for the invasion of the Soviet Union stimulated a growth in both the number and size of Army and Waffen-SS units. Three new *Totenkopf* Regiments were raised from the 40,000 members of the Totenkopfstandarten not already integrated in the *Totenkopf* Division, and these formed the nucleus for Kampfgruppe (later Division) *Nord*, while the *Germania* Regiment was detached from the SS-V (itself now renamed *Deutschland,* then *Reich,* later *Das Reich*) to form the nucleus of a new Germanic Division, originally called *Germania* but soon changed to *Wiking*, which drew on volunteers from occupied territories for its manpower.

The Waffen-SS order of battle at the beginning of the Balkan campaign which preceded the invasion of Russia in April 1941 thus stood at: the Leibstandarte *Adolf Hitler*; SS Division *Reich*; SS *Totenkopf* Division; SS Polizei Division; SS Division *Wiking*; SS Kampfgruppe *Nord*; and SS Standarte Nr 9 (a Totenkopf unit). Each regiment had a reserve battalion in Germany which was intended to supply trained troops as casualty replacements. In addition, the five remaining Totenkopfstandarten were drawn together

Above left *Himmler congratulates Hausser on the performance of the SS troops at the conclusion of the campaign in the west. Ostendorff, who was on Hausser's staff at the time, is in the centre, with no collar insignia (81/146/11A).*

Above and right *A parade of the Leibstandarte down the Champs Elysées. Here a StuG III passes the reviewing stand . . . (75/119/19) . . . watched by Sepp Dietrich (in helmet), von Rundstedt (centre) and Paul Hausser (75/119/18).*

in a training area around Debica, in Poland, where two of them were turned into cavalry regiments (to form the nucleus of the later SS Kavallerie Division *Florian Geyer*), the remainder forming two unnamed motorised brigades. Three new police regiments, at this time separate from the Waffen-SS, were also raised by Himmler, principally for behind the lines and anti-partisan duties.

On December 18 1940 Hitler issued his first directive for Operation Barbarossa—the invasion of Russia—but this was to be forestalled, with devastating consequences, by the failure of Hitler's ally, Mussolini, in the Balkans. The Italians had, without German sanction, invaded Greece in October 1940, and rapidly proved themselves inadequate to the task, even before the Empire Expeditionary Force landed to assist the Greeks in March 1941.

Under heavy political pressure, Bulgaria and then Yugoslavia were forced to declare themselves on the German side, although the latter was only a temporary state of affairs because the Yugoslav

Above left *Leibstandarte Marder IIs (PzKpfw II chassis with 7.5 cm Pak 40) approach the Arc de Triomphe* (75/119/20).
Above right *A PzKpfw IVF2 passes the Arc de Triomphe* (75/119/21).

government was overthrown and a new, anti-German, regime repudiated the alliance. Hitler, in one of the hysterical rages for which he became infamous, declared the postponement of the Russian campaign in order to crush these dissidents.

Leibstandarte and *Reich* moved from their rest areas in France and Austria into Rumania in preparation for the invasion of Yugoslavia, *Reich* under the command of Reinhardt's XLI Panzer Korps, Leibstandarte in List's XII Army. *Reich* distinguished itself immediately following the invasion of Yugoslavia on April 6, Paul Hausser describing their operations in the following words[*]:

'The operation against Belgrade, the capital city, started with the main troop concentration south of the rivers Drau and Danube. Only Reinhardt's

Panzer Korps was employed north of the rivers for mopping up in the Banat and Batschka provinces. It seemed hopeless to try and reach Belgrade from north of the Danube. Nevertheless, an assault party under Hauptsturmführer Fritz Klingenberg of the motor cycle battalion got hold of a motor boat and, after a hazardous journey, managed to enter Belgrade and force the mayor to hand over the city.'

The Leibstandarte, meanwhile, had been involved in very stiff fighting in the mountains guarding the Yugoslav-Greek border, taking two days to force the Klidi Pass against stubborn Australian and New Zealand resistance, and then the Klissura Pass against the Greeks. During part of the latter assault Kurt 'Panzer' Meyer, who was then in command of the reconnaissance battalion, had to throw a hand grenade at the heels of his own troops to force them into the open against heavy machine-gun fire. This

[*]*Waffen im Einsatz*—see bibliography.

Hitler's Samurai

questionable action nevertheless resulted in over a thousand prisoners for the loss of only six Leibstandarte troopers killed and nine wounded. Meyer himself said later that 'never again did I witness such a concerted leap forward as at that second!' A day later his unorthodox methods were further rewarded by the capture of another 11,000 prisoners, for which he received the Knight's Cross. Next, the Leibstandarte captured another mountain pass, the Metzovon, cutting off 16 Greek divisions and forcing them to surrender. Greece capitulated three days later and the British Empire Expeditionary Force had to retreat, narrowly avoiding being cut off by a daring Fallschirmjäger assault on the Corinth Canal.

However brilliant and successful the initial Balkan campaign had been, however, it had delayed the planned invasion of Russia by over a month. Some subsequent historians have attempted to pass this off as irrelevant, saying that Hitler's later decision to divert Army Group Centre to the Kiev front, instead of allowing it to press on to Moscow, would have happened all the same and would have been equally decisive; while Soviet historians have always denied that the weather played any part in the German forces' failure to capture the capital. Personally, while recognising that both of these arguments contain strong elements of truth, I am convinced that it was the late start to the campaign, and the early onset of a particularly fierce winter, which more than anything else prevented the Germans from achieving their initial objectives. Even if these had not forced an immediate capitulation, they would have seriously hindered the transfer of Soviet war production further east and delayed the rapid Russian arms build-up which led inexorably to the disaster of VI Army at Stalingrad, the stalemate at Kursk and the inevitable German defeat.

Nevertheless, the real saga of the Waffen-SS was played out in Russia, hence the preponderance of Eastern Front photographs in this book. As Heinz Höhne, who is far from an SS apologist, says*: in Russia the SS soldiers found themselves 'living in another world, a cruel remorseless world, aeons removed from the ideological verbiage of the SS. Driven by belief in their Führer and in the ultimate victory of Germany, the SS formations stormed

*The Order of the Death's Head—see bibliography.

Fritz Klingenberg at the time of his audacious thrust on Belgrade (75/120/16A).

through the steppes, marshes and forests of Russia, both heroes and victims of a ghastly chapter of human error and hallucination. They won for themselves a select place in the annals of war. Wherever in the south, the centre or the north, wherever the enemy recovered sufficiently from his surprise to stand and fight, wherever he launched a counter-attack and tore gaps in the German attacking front, orders went out for the SS formations'.

The front-line strength of the Waffen-SS on June 22 1941 is given in a statistical report to Himmler dated August 27 the same year: 10,796 men in the Leibstandarte *Adolf Hitler*; 19,021 in *Reich*; 18,754 in *Totenkopf*; 17,347 in Polizei: 10,573 in *Nord*; and 19,377 in *Wiking*. In addition, there were 904 Finnish volunteers in the *Nordost* Battalion, 29,809 men in the reserve battalions, and others totalling in all 160,405 men in staff, administrative, concentration camp, guard and garrison posts and the officer and NCO training schools.

Nord, and the SS Standarte Nr 9, fought in the far north, on the Finnish front; *Totenkopf*, with Polizei as a reserve, fought with Army Group North in the drive towards Leningrad; *Reich* was with Army Group Centre in its initial drive towards Moscow; and Leibstandarte *Adolf Hitler* and *Wiking* were with Army Group South.

The war in the east was seen by the SS at the time—and in post-war propaganda—as a great crusade to save the west from 'Asiatic Communism'. By its very nature it was therefore bound to be one of the most bitter, viciously contested campaigns in history, with higher casualties and greater atrocities on both sides than ever seen before. Himmler, amongst his milder ravings, said in a speech to men of Kampfgruppe *Nord*: 'When you, my men, fight over there in the East, you are carrying on the same struggle, against the same subhumanity, the same inferior races, that at one time appeared under the name of Huns, another time—1,000 years ago, at the time of King Henry and Otto I—under the name of Magyars, another time under the name of Tartars, and still another time under the name of Genghis Khan and the Mongols. Today they appear as Russians under the political banner of Bolshevism'.

Yet tens of thousands of these 'subhumans' were soon to join the ranks of the Waffen-SS!

At this point it is necessary briefly to look at the structure and activities of the Einsatzgruppen, the extermination squads which followed the invading armies into the field and whose sole objective was the wholesale slaughter of the Jews. Formed by Heydrich, they comprised some 3,000 men in four groups of roughly battalion size. And, although Waffen-SS apologists have tried to deny any link between the Waffen-SS and these murder squads, the simple fact is that over a third (34 per cent) of their strength was drawn from the ranks of existing Waffen-SS formations. Moving close behind the advancing front line so that few could evade their net, the Einsatzgruppen brutally shot, bayoneted, burnt, tortured, clubbed to death or buried alive almost half a million Jews in the first six months of the campaign. Details are available elsewhere for those with the stomach to read them. People were shot in the stomach to die in agony while their exterminators stood around joking and taking bets on how long they would last; babies had their heads smashed against walls to save ammunition; nobody was safe. Yet even the men of the Einsatzgruppen sickened of the horror, von dem Bach-Zelewski himself suffering a nervous breakdown and others

Waffen-SS motor cyclists cross the Russian frontier (marked by the striped column on the right) (75/120/25A).

committing suicide through a surfeit of guilt. When Himmler attended the execution of 200 Jews in Minsk, even he was so revolted at the carnage that he ordered a new method to be found. From this stemmed the gas trucks and the later ovens.

The men of the Einsatzgruppen used all manner of psychological tricks to persuade themselves that what they were doing was 'right' after basic ideology failed. The Jews were not just civilians, but partisans, arsonists, saboteurs, couriers, spies and criminals. Later, the Einsatzgruppen were actually to fight in an anti-partisan role as the Army (which cannot therefore absolve itself of guilt either) found their activities so 'useful'. Halder, the Army Chief of Staff in December 1941, said: 'these people [the Einsatzgruppen] are worth their weight in gold to us. They guarantee the security of our rear communications and so save us calling upon troops for this purpose'.

Apologists who deny that the Waffen-SS or the Army knew of the Einsatzgruppen activities must, therefore, have been deaf as well as blind and, ultimately, dumb.

Returning to the main course of the Russian campaign, *Nord* began by disgracing itself. During an assault on a Russian stronghold in concert with German and Finnish Army troops, they were forced back twice with heavy casualties and many SS men panicked, throwing away their weapons and running headlong back through their own lines. Elsewhere, however, the Waffen-SS formations fought hard and creditably, although *Totenkopf* and Polizei saw less action initially, being mainly used as reserve formations in support of Army Group North's drive towards Leningrad. In the centre, however, *Reich* was very heavily involved. Klingenberg, the hero of Belgrade, was successful in establishing the first bridgehead over the River Beresina. The division then provided flank guard during the drive on Smolensk, in company with the Army's premier division, *Grossdeutschland**, and the 10th Panzer Division. Spearheading a drive south of Smolensk, *Reich* became involved in very heavy fighting around Yelnya, where Klingenberg again distinguished himself and earned a specific mention in Guderian's memoirs. For a month the division was left virtually

*Often referred to as an SS unit by writers of popular fiction! For full details see Osprey's 'Vanguard' title by Bruce Quarrie.

to its own devices holding the flank of Guderian's Army Group while it was diverted to help seal the Kiev pocket, suffering appalling casualties against odds, on occasion, of 11 to one. In August they were withdrawn for a rest.

Meanwhile, the Leibstandarte *Adolf Hitler* and *Wiking* had also been distinguishing themselves in the south. From their start line near Lublin, in Poland, they forced their way south, the Leibstandarte through Ostrog and the Wiking through Tarnopol, swinging north to Zhitomir, south-west of Kiev, then on through Uman down the eastern bank of the River Bug towards the Crimea. Breaking through the Soviet defences at Perekop, they pushed on through Taganrog as far as Rostov-on-Don, on the Black Sea coast. In the fighting around Archangelsk the Leibstandarte earned the outspoken gratitude of the Korps commander, Kempf. Writing afterwards, he said: 'committed at the focus of the battle for the seizure of (this) key enemy position, the Leibstandarte . . . with incomparable dash, took the city and the heights to the south. In the spirit of the most devoted brotherhood of arms, they intervened on their own initiative in the arduous struggle of the 16th Infantry Division on their left flank and routed the enemy, destroying numerous tanks'. Similarly, the *Wiking* Division even earned the accolade of the Russian Major-General Artemenko who, when captured, said that the Soviet forces had 'breathed a sigh of relief' when the division was relieved by Army units, and that *Wiking* had shown 'greater fortitude' than any other formation on either side.

While *Das Reich* (after another change of name) was pushing on to Moscow, eventually coming to within 6 km of the city centre, the Leibstandarte had established a bridgehead across the River Dnieper. But now the weather intervened. Rain and mud in October, followed by cold and snow in November, accompanied by increasing Russian resistance and counter-attacks, halted the advance. The appalling conditions forced the Leibstandarte to withdraw, although they held the line at Dnepropetrovsk in February 1942 against a concerted Russian attack until other units could be thrown in to relieve them. The Russians also counter-attacked around Moscow, where *Das Reich* endured over 4,000 casualties in heavy defensive fighting throughout the winter. Due to these, the division was withdrawn from the line in March and returned to France for rest and refit

Infantry in snow camouflage, winter 1941. The foreground man is firing an Erma EMP 9 mm SMG (81/143/24A).

which lasted until July, followed by occupation duties until it was returned to the Russian front at the beginning of 1943.

The Leibstandarte and *Wiking* Divisions remained in the line, the former until August 1942 when, after severe defensive fighting in the Donets region, it, too, was returned for rest and refit as a Panzer division; the latter staying on to achieve further fame by reaching the far Caucasus Mountains in the autumn. Meanwhile, *Totenkopf* had also experienced heavy fighting in the Demyansk pocket which lasted throughout most of 1942 until it, too, was withdrawn to be re-formed as a Panzer division.

Nord, which had been withdrawn following its ignominious rout at Salla, had been re-formed and retrained as a mountain division, returning to the Finnish front in August 1942. The Polizei Division, which had fought quite well on the Wolchow River during the desperate days of January-March 1942, went back into reserve as a security force until June 1943, when it joined the SS-Freiwilligen Gebirgs Division *Prinz Eugen* in anti-partisan duties in the Balkans.

Prinz Eugen itself began forming in March 1942, from 'ethnic' Germans, principally in Rumania, becoming operational in October of that year. Similarly, the *Totenkopf* cavalry Standarten referred to above were formed into a mobile anti-partisan force behind the lines in Russia from August 1941-June 1942. They then spent two months being raised in strength to a division, fighting in the Vyazma-Bryansk-Rzhev salient throughout the winter of 1942-43.

At the beginning of 1943 the situation in Russia looked extremely bleak. Von Paulus' VI Army had fallen in Stalingrad and a headlong Soviet offensive had carried the Russians as far west as Kharkov. However, they were over-extended. The newly formed SS Panzer Korps, comprising the three re-formed SS Panzer Divisions Leibstandarte *Adolf Hitler*, *Das Reich* and *Totenkopf*, had returned to the front in February and were badly mauled during the Russian attack on the city. However, ignoring one of Hitler's 'hold at all costs' orders, they had fallen back to regroup and, on February 23, began a vigorous counter-attack of their own. In this, one of the classic operations of the war, they destroyed over 600 tanks and left 20,000 Russian dead on the 50-mile battlefield. The Panzer Korps had vindicated its stroke. However, the cost had been high—a total of

The battle for Kharkov was the first real triumph for the SS Panzer Korps. This picture shows Leibstandarte PzKpfw IIIs on the outskirts of the city (75/119/25).

12,000 dead and wounded.

While both sides paused for breath during that hot, dusty summer of 1943 prior to the biggest single battle of the war, and the biggest tank battle of all time until the Arab-Israeli War of 1973, further SS units were constantly being formed. These included the 9th SS Panzer Division *Hohenstaufen*, under Wilhelm Bittrich, which spent the year working up; the 10th, *Frundsberg,* under Brigadeführer Debes; the 12th *Hitlerjugend*, under Brigadeführer Witt; and several of the more suspect formations, such as the 13th, *Handschar*, recruited from Bosnian Moslems; the Ukrainian 14th and others discussed in chapter two; plus the 16th, *Reichsführer-SS*, raised from Himmler's own personal guard battalion to the size of a brigade in February 1943 and to that of a division in October.

After the German counter-offensive at Kharkov ended, the Germans had created a salient whose eastern edge was the River Donets and whose apex was Belgorod, pointing into the Russian lines. To the north of this was another salient around Orel. In

between these two 'fingers', however, was a Soviet 'fist', a large bulge into German-occupied territory centred on a small town which most people had never heard of—Kursk. The German intention was to pinch off this Russian salient and straighten their own lines prior to a renewed push eastwards. However, the Russians saw it as an ideal platform for a renewed offensive themselves. And so a massive build-up began on both sides.

In the northern salient, the Germans placed II Panzer Army and IX Army; in the southern, Kampfgruppe Kempf and IV Panzer Army, including the three premier SS Panzer Divisions. The two-pronged attack, codenamed *Zitadelle* (Citadel), appeared to begin well, the strong Panzer forces in the south making excellent headway for a few miles. But the Russians were present in such strength, with such well-laid minefields and anti-tank batteries with overlapping fields of fire, that the most heroic efforts were in vain and, as the Soviet pressure increased, even the SS Panzer Korps, its ranks practically decimated, had to give ground. Moreover, the Allies had just landed in Sicily, and Hitler decided to send the Leibstandarte there post-haste. (Its departure was shortlived, for within three months the situation in Russia had become so desperate that it was recalled.)

Das Reich *trucks and half-tracks (note the special 'Kursk' divisional marking)* (81/143/3A).

From this point on, despite many successful local counter-attacks, the Germans were on the defensive in Russia. And, just as they had spearheaded the advances, so too did the Waffen-SS formations shore up the defences in the most critical sectors. In November it was the Leibstandarte which successfully hurled the Russians back around Kiev. But it was the SS divisions' turn to be encircled next, as they had helped to encircle so many Russian armies. In December the Russians struck at Army Group Centre, smashing through in a parallel of the classic German blitzkrieg manoeuvres of the early war years, overrunning the defences around Kiev and reaching the pre-war Polish frontier. They also struck in the north, forcing the Germans to give up the epic siege of Leningrad.

Wiking, along with two Army Corps, was entrapped in February in the vicinity of Cherkassy, and Leibstandarte plus 2,500 men from *Das Reich*

were similarly caught in the Kamenets-Podolsk pocket. After two weeks in their steadily shrinking perimeter, *Wiking* spearheaded a breakout which was only successful at the expense of all the division's tanks and half its troops. No such escape was possible for the forces trapped around Kamenets-Podolsk, so the newly operational 9th and 10th SS Panzer Divisions *Hohenstaufen* and *Frundsberg* were assigned to their rescue. Despite appalling conditions, they succeeded in breaking through the surrounding Soviet lines and clearing a path through which I Panzer Army could escape.

The tattered remnants of the proud Leibstandarte were sent back to Belgium to lick their wounds and refit; the *Das Reich* survivors were sent to rejoin the rest of their divisional comrades in France. From north to south, the SS divisions now in the front line on the Eastern Front were as follows: *Nord* in Finland; *Nordland* and *Niederland* in the Baltic;

Hitler's Samurai

Hohenstaufen, *Frundsberg* and the survivors of *Wiking* (re-formed into a 4,000-strong Kampfgruppe) in Poland; and *Totenkopf* in the south. But now further SS formations were brought into play. *Reichsführer-SS* (leaving some of its units in Italy), *Horst Wessel* and *Florian Geyer* were assigned to a pre-emptive invasion of Hungary. But two hammer blows were about to bring the Third Reich to its knees.

On June 6 1944 the Allied invasion of Normandy, Operation *Overlord*, took place; and, just over a fortnight later, the Russians launched their own summer offensive. Apart from the Leibstandarte and *Das Reich*, the only other two SS divisions available to meet the Allied invasion were *Hitlerjugend* and *Götz von Berlichingen*; however, *Hohenstaufen* and *Frundsberg* were hastily recalled.

It will be remembered that the *Totenkopf* and Leibstandarte had both committed atrocities during the fighting in France and Belgium in 1940; now it was the turn of *Das Reich*. During the division's march to the front, a company of the *Der Führer* Regiment, commanded by Sturmbannführer Dickmann, massacred 642 men, women and children at Oradour-sur-Glane in supposed reprisal for a sniper firing at them. The unblooded *Hitlerjugend* Division also tarnished its escutcheon within ten days of the Normandy landings. Sixty-four Canadian and British prisoners, many of them wounded, were wantonly shot. 'Panzer' Meyer was later condemned to death for this by a Canadian tribunal, but the sentence was commuted and he was released from jail in 1954.

All the SS divisions distinguished themselves in the Normandy fighting, however. A first British attempt, headed by the 51st Highland Division, to break out near Caen, was thwarted by the Leibstandarte and *Das Reich*, supported by *Hohenstaufen* and *Frundsberg* which came in on the flank. Three weeks later Montgomery tried again, in an operation codenamed *Goodwood*. During the course of this, one of the most famous tank engagements of the war took place, when Germany's Panzer 'ace', Michael Wittman, with his own and three other Tiger tanks plus a PzKpfw IV, stopped a column of 7th Armoured Division Cromwells at Villers-Bocage, causing such demoralisation that the attack was called off. (Wittman was killed on August 8 when his Tiger was destroyed by the concerted fire of five

Shermans. His body lay in an anonymous grave until 1983 when it was re-interred with proper honours at La Cambe.)

From this point on, however, even the determination of the SS divisions could not stem the tide. A few days after *Goodwood*, Patton's tanks succeeded in breaking out of the bridgehead in the direction of Avranches and St Lô. A counter-attack was hastily prepared, involving not only the Leibstandarte and *Das Reich*, but also *Hohenstaufen*, *Frundsberg*, *Götz von Berlichingen* and three Army divisions. This time the Americans were not to be stopped. Devastating air attacks broke up the Panzers and, although they continued stubbornly to resist, the remainder of the German forces were, to quote Eisenhower, 'in a state of complete disorganisation'. Now, too, the élite SS divisions were in dire danger of falling prey to an Allied encirclement, the British from the north and the Americans from the south, in the Falaise pocket. It was only the staunch 18-year-olds of the *Hitlerjugend* Division who held the neck of the pocket open long enough to allow the tattered remnants of the other divisions to escape.

Meanwhile, in Russia the German front line resembled a colander, the summer offensive having broken it virtually everywhere. There was no remaining cohesion, only isolated pockets still holding out. Among these were *Totenkopf* and *Wiking*, who threw back the initial Soviet attempt to capture Warsaw for sufficiently long to enable von dem Bach-Zelewski to crush the Warsaw Uprising with his customary brutality. In fact, *Totenkopf* and *Wiking* brought the German forces in the east a badly needed breathing space in which to shorten their lines and regroup, for the Russians now found themselves over-extended (having advanced some 500 km in five weeks) and were not able to renew the attack until January 1945.

In the west, the Allies encountered the same problem. Having reached the Seine and liberated Paris, they, too, were over-extended, and their tanks had insufficient petrol to continue the advance. Most of the SS divisions had been withdrawn to Germany following the Normandy fighting, and would shortly take part in Hitler's last desperate gamble to reverse his fortunes in the west. But, unknown to Allied planners, *Hohenstaufen* and *Frundsberg* had retired to Arnhem to rest and refit, and were thus able to be largely instrumental in defeating Montgomery's ambitious airborne operation, *Market-Garden*, to force an early crossing of the Rhine.

As their supplies gradually caught up with them, the Allies had continued to advance, and Hitler now assembled his last hope. The Leibstandarte, *Das Reich* and *Hitlerjugend*, together with *Hohenstaufen*, fresh from the fighting in Holland, formed the spearhead of a new VI Panzer Army which, together with Army formations, hoped to repeat the surprise attack through the Ardennes which had led to the Allied defeat in 1940. To begin with they made good progress, largely because bad weather prevented the Allies getting adequate air support into the area. But the attack became bogged down, the tanks being unable to move at more than a crawl on the treacherously icy roads and, when the skies cleared, air attacks kept the German heads down and made movement impossible.

In desperation Hitler threw more units into another offensive in Alsace, where the American line had been denuded in order to send troops to the Ardennes. Led by *Götz von berlichingen*, this was no more successful, even when *Frundsberg* and *Nord* were thrown in as reserves.

Of all the Waffen-SS atrocities, the one which arouses the strongest feelings and the greatest controversy took place during the Ardennes offensive. Some 90 American soldiers had been captured by Joachim Peiper's advance guard of the Leibstandarte—but this is about the only point on which sources agree. Peiper himself asserted at his trial that, after disarming them, being unable to cope with prisoners because of his task, he sent them marching towards the rear where they attempted to give themselves up to the main force of the Leibstandarte but were shot down in mistake. The story told by American survivors differs. To begin with, their testimony at Nürnberg places the original number of prisoners as far higher than the number of bodies plus eventual survivors could account for ('maybe 175 men' according to the only officer to survive). This suggests the possibility that there could be an element of truth in some German accounts which suggest that some of the prisoners tried to escape after surrendering to Peiper. What *is* incontestable, however, is the fact that 71 prisoners were machine-gunned to death, but by precisely which unit of the Leibstandarte will probably never now be proven. After the war, both Peiper and

Dietrich, the Army commander, accepted responsibility for the massacre, although both denied any direct complicity. Both were sentenced to death, alongside the divisional commander, Hermann Priess, but all sentences were commuted. Peiper, the last to be released from prison, in 1956, received many death threats after his return to Stuttgart and eventually went into hiding under an assumed name in France. He was murdered in 1976, his assassins remaining so far uncaught although it is probably safe to assume that the hunt was none too vigorous.

Following the abortive Ardennes offensive, popularly known as the 'Battle of the Bulge', Hitler's attention became distracted to Hungary, where the IX SS Korps, which included *Florian Geyer* and the 22nd SS Freiwilligen Kavallerie Division, had been cut off in Budapest. Determined to rescue them, Hitler detached *Totenkopf* and *Wiking* from Warsaw. Predictably, the attempt was doomed to failure, despite two week's hard fighting.

Now, on January 12 1945, the Russians launched their long-expected final assault, and the race for Berlin was on. Suicidally, Hitler persisted in his attempt to relieve Budapest, and turned the remnants of VI Panzer Army towards Hungary. However, the entrapped SS troops did not know of this and made a hopeless attempt to break out on their own, at attempt which only 785 men from an original 50,000 survived. Nevertheless, the battered VI Panzer Army, reinforced by the *Reichsführer-SS*, made a valiant attempt to stem the Russian tide, but by March all were in retreat. When he heard the news, Hitler was enraged. Even his beloved SS was failing him now. He ordered the men of VI Panzer Army to remove their proud cuff titles as they were no longer entitled to them. Bitterly, Sepp Dietrich commented 'that's your reward for all you've done these last five years'. But the game was almost played out. The last act went to Felix Steiner, who had gathered the remnants of the once proud formations *Frundsberg*, Polizei, *Nordland*, *Niederland* and *Wallonien* around him for the final, last-ditch defence of Berlin. Ordered to counter-attack against the Russians, Steiner obeyed orders to the end, and tried. And, of course, failed. So, while the last survivors, loyal to their honour to the bitter end, fought in the burning ruins, their insane Führer committed suicide, bringing to a finish one of the most terrible holocausts in history.

This photograph *Men of the* Totenkopf *Standarte* Oberbayern *drag an assault boat up to a waterway, possibly the La Bassée Canal, during the invasion of the west, May 1940 (81/142/14).*
Below Totenkopf *Division pioneers at work repairing a bridge over the La Bassée Canal, May 29 1940 (81/142/12).*

Left *A broken-down Mercedes truck of the* Totenkopf *Division in the south of France, June 1940. Note one of the many variants of the death's head device on the mudguard (81/142/9).*

Below *An anti-tank detachment of the SS-Verfügungs Division in France. The gun is a Pak 35/36 (81/141/25).*

Right *Mounted Army personnel walk past an SS-V car in France (81/146/2A).*

Below right *SS-V personnel examine a knocked-out British tank during the advance towards the coast (81/146/3A).*

Opposite page *Dramatic sequence showing a French Hotchkiss H-39 being hit and destroyed by close-range anti-tank fire during the campaign in the west. Bundesarchiv records identify this incident as occurring on May 20 1940 near Arras (81/142/15-17).*

Above right *Manoeuvring a light artillery piece by hand (81/146/13A).*

Right *Officers watch a Pak 35/36 drill aboard one of the landing barges prior to the invasion which never happened—that of England. These are SS-V troops (81/146/15A).*

Right *Smiling Reich soldiers during the triumphant entry into Belgrade (75/120/15A).*

Heydrich and Himmler in Prague, October 29 1941 (72/39/24A).

Top *Infantry of* Reich *marching through one of the seemingly endless Russian forests* (73/83/50).
Above *PzKpfw IIIFs of* Reich *during the summer of 1941* (75/120/31A).

Hitler's Samurai

Top *An SS motor cycle combination passes a column of* Reich *SdKfz 231 armoured cars* (75/120/24A).
Above *A* Reich *PzKpfw III seen from a truck during the advance* (75/120/27A).

The Waffen-SS at war

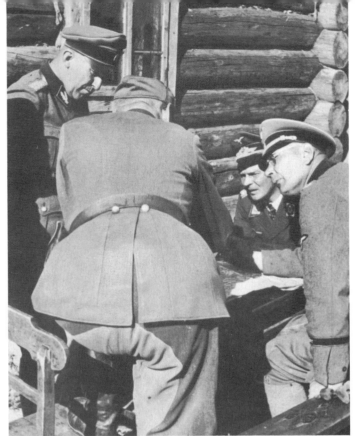

Left *High-level conference at* Totenkopf *headquarters during the summer of 1941. On the left is Oberführer Matthias Kleinheisterkamp. With back to camera is von Manstein, facing von Richthofen, while on the right is Georg Keppler (81/146/6A).*

Below Totenkopf *trucks on a dusty Russian road, July 23 1941 (81/142/1).*

Right *A Russian peasant pours a glass of milk for a soldier from the* Westland *Regiment (81/144/1A).*

Below *A* Totenkopf *Feldlazarette (81/142/3).*

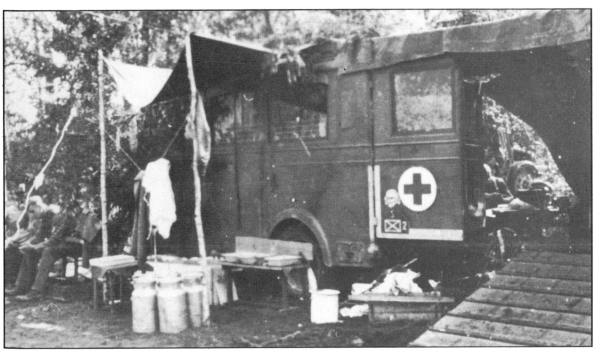

Above *A bicycle built for two—SS engineers in Karelia with boxes of equipment on the backs (81/141/22).*

Left *Men of the SS Kavallerie Brigade mount up (75/118/4).*

Above right *An SS Kavallerie Brigade MG 34 team in action (75/118/5).*

Right *Another way of using the MG 34! (75/120/2A).*

Above *A Hauptsturmführer of the* Totenkopf *Division wearing a sniper's mask pushed back over his helmet* (75/118/11).

Right *Looking like creatures from a science-fiction movie, an MG 34 team with face masks and extensive foliage tied on to their helmets* (75/120/10A).

Above Reich *troops wait for the order to move* (75/120/35A).

Above right *A non-regulation accessory being carried by a man of the* Totenkopf *Division* (81/141/10).

Right *One would have thought mittens impractical in combat, but during the first Russian winter German troops acquired whatever warm clothing they could find. The man on the right is wearing a rubberised motor cycle coat* (75/119/3A).

Far right *Winter arrives, but Fritz Klingenberg (now wearing the Knight's Cross he was awarded for the capture of Belgrade) seems unperturbed* (75/119/2A).

Left *A* Reich *patrol. The man standing on the right wears his camouflage smock over his greatcoat, while he on the left has lightweight snow camouflage over his (75/119/11).*

Below left *Fritz Christen, then aged 20, was the first and the youngest enlisted man in the Waffen-SS to win the Knight's Cross when, on October 20 1941, as a Sturmann in charge of a Pak 38, he single-handedly destroyed 13 Soviet tanks (81/143/26A).*

Below *Winter 1941-42. Map reading instruction for a trainee* Totenkopf *despatch rider in France (81/141/30).*

Right *A wooden-roofed dugout provides some shelter from the elements for soldiers of the* Reich Division. *In the background is what appears to be an old Russian monastery (75/119/13).*

Below right *PzKpfw IIIL of the* Wiking *Division during the winter of 1941-42 (81/144/22A).*

Opposite page and above *Cross-country training for more* Totenkopf *personnel in France during the winter of 1941-42* (81/141/31, 32 & 34).
Below Totenkopf *troops practice with an MG 34 on its tripod in the sustained fire role* (81/141/35).

Above *When the spring thaw came in Russia, streams turned into torrents, as this* Wiking *Division truck has found* (81/141/7).

Left and opposite page *Leibstandarte PzKpfw IVF2s shortly after the division was equipped with them in France, July 1942 (75/119/15-17).*

Above left *A PzKpfw III of the* Wiking *Division clearly showing the divisional insignia, summer 1942* (75/118/26).

Above *Grenadiers of the* Wiking *Division's* Germania *Regiment in the summer of 1942* (75/118/27).

Left *Sturmbannführer Max Seela, who won the Knight's Cross in Russia on May 3 1942 as CO of the 3rd Company, SS Pionier Bataillon,* Totenkopf *Division* (75/118/13).

Above right *Amphibious Volkswagen 'jeeps' of* Das Reich, *summer 1942* (75/119/22).

Right *With frame radio aerial folded flat, this is an SdKfz 260 or 261 of the* Wiking *Division (*Germania *Regiment) in Russia, 1942* (75/118/29).

Left *Untersturmführer August Zingel, CO of an assault group formed from the 15th Company of the Totenkopf's 1st Infantry Regiment. He won the Knight's Cross on September 5 1942 for continuing to lead an attack although wounded (75/118/10).*

Below *An SS PzKpfw IV in Russia, autumn 1942 (81/144/2A).*

Right *A* Totenkopf *15 cm sFH 18 in action during the summer of 1942. The crew are wearing sports shorts in the heat (75/118/7).*

Below right *Sepp Dietrich (on the left of photo) with other Leibstandarte officers in Kharkov (75/119/23).*

Above *A Leibstandarte MG 42 team, wearing parkas, hitch a lift on a PzKpfw IV (75/119/27).*

Left *Paul Hausser in the turret of a* Das Reich *PzKpfw III during the battle for Kharkov (81/142/29).*

Above right *Leibstandarte SdKfz 251 half-tracks in Kharkov (75/119/29).*

Right *All wearing parkas, soldiers of the Leibstandarte snatch a cigarette break during the heavy fighting for the city (75/119/32).*

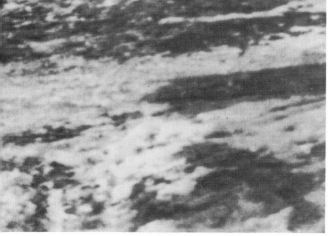

Above *A Leibstandarte PzKpfw IVG with, in background, a light SdKfz 250 half-track (75/120/8A).*

Left Totenkopf *infantry ride on a PzKpfw IV through the recaptured city (81/141/23).* **Inset** Totenkopf *tank commanders confer. Note the Untersturmführer on the right wears a sleeveless sheepskin jerkin over his black Panzer jacket (75/119/28).*

Below *A* Totenkopf *Tiger tank during the battle for Kharkov (75/118/14).*

Far left *Himmler flew out personally to congratulate the men of schwere Panzer Abteilung 502,* Das Reich*'s Tiger tank unit, in April 1943 (75/120/37).*

Left *Himmler inspects* Das Reich *armoured troops. In the background is a Tiger, in front of that a PzKpfw IVG, while the barrel in the foreground appears to be from a self-propelled gun (81/142/31).*

Below left *Walter Krüger addresses sPzAbt 502, April 20 1943 (75/119/36).*

Right *The Knight's Cross for Standartenführer Gustav Lombard, CO of* Florian Geyer*'s 1st Kavallerie Regiment, in March 1943. Lombard was responsible for the killing of an unknown number of Soviet partisans while working with Fegelein. He was later captured by the Russians but, surprisingly, was released by them in 1955 (81/141/16).*

Below *SS armour in Kharkov after the fighting, circa May 1943. On the left is a PzKpfw III and on the right a Tiger in yellow paint scheme with green camouflage (81/142/33).*

Hitler's Samurai

Left *A convoy of* Totenkopf *vehicles entrained for the front* (81/145/14).

Below left *Men of an SS light flak detachment race to their 2 cm gun* (81/142/2).

Right *Operation Citadel—the battle of Kursk. Loading ammunition into a* Das Reich Panther (81/144/14A).

Below Das Reich *Panthers camouflaged on the steppes* (81/144/13A).

Left Totenkopf *infantry confer with a Tiger commander during the battle* (81/144/16A).

Below left *A* Totenkopf *PzKpfw III* (75/118/16).

Bottom left *A* Totenkopf *Tiger tank* (75/118/15).

Top Right *A pause in the fighting for the crew of a Totenkopf SdKfz 250/1* (81/143/20A).

Above right *Unterscharführer Johann Thaler won the Knight's Cross during the battle of Kursk as a PzKpfw IV driver in* Das Reich. *Note that several of the admiring men around him are wearing the lightweight camouflaged drill uniform* (81/143/19A).

Right *Latvian volunteers in action, summer 1943* (81/142/34).

Above *Tigers and PzKpfw IVs of* Das Reich *during the autumn of 1943 (81/142/27).*

Left *Tying their weapons together before ascending a rock face are men of the Prinz Eugen Division in the Balkans, 1943 (81/141/18).*

Above right *SS infantry storm a defended building (75/118/36).*

Right *Men of the* Totenkopf *Division with a field telephone, September/October 1943 (75/118/20).*

Above left *Hermann Priess, commander of Toten-kopf in September/October 1943. He had taken over the division when Eicke was killed. He was later indicted in the Malmedy trial but eventually released (75/118/19).*

Above *Sturmann Remy Schrÿnen, left, a member of the Langemark Division, on his award of the Knight's Cross for single-handedly knocking out seven Soviet tanks even though wounded. Accompanying him is Untersturmführer Koslovsky (Christopher Ailsby Photographic Collection).*

Left *A Waffen-SS cine cameraman wearing the SS-Kriegsberichter armband (81/143/27A).*

Above right *The long retreat—a StuG III in the ruins of a Russian town (75/118/21).*

Right *Wiking Division troops in snow camouflage with a StuG III (SdKfz 142/2) mounting a 10.5 cm StuH 42 in Saukopf mantlet (81/144/26A).*

Above *Wiking Division PzKpfw IVs near Kowel, March 1944; the Russians were using Lease-Lend Shermans in this engagement (81/144/27A).*

Right *Outside Warsaw in 1944—a* Wiking *Division Tiger (695/406/13A).*

Hitler's Samurai

Below *Just before the end—Totenkopf troops shelter behind a knocked-out T-34, autumn 1944 (24/3535/23).*

Right *Infantry and Panther tanks of the* Wiking *Division in May 1944 (81/144/30A).*

Below right *The Warsaw butcher—Obergruppenführer Erich von dem Bach-Zelewskim who saved his own neck by giving evidence for the prosecution at Nürnberg and thereby avoiding extradition to Poland. He lived until 1972 (81/148/13).*

Appendices

1. The Britische Freikorps

Originally known as the Legion of St George, the *Britische Freikorps* was formed predominantly from prewar Mosleyite blackshirts or from men in the British armed forces who had divided loyalties because of a German parent. Many of them genuinely believed that Britain's fight should be against Communism rather than against National Socialism, but others were just 'cowboys'.

The concept of the Korps originated with John Amery, eldest son of a distinguished British Peer. Unable to persuade Wehrmacht authorities of the feasibility of recruiting from British prisoners of war, he approached Gottlob Berger after the latter had started his SS enlistment drive in occupied countries. It met with very limited success. An early recruit was 'Frank Wood' (all members of the Freikorps used pseudonyms), a former Lancashire pharmacist, and it was he who drafted the 'Fellow Countrymen!' leaflet which was distributed through PoW camps. An even earlier member was Thomas Mellor Cooper, whose mother was German and who had joined the SS in 1938, fighting with *Das Reich* in Russia and being awarded the wound badge in black (the only Englishman to receive a Nazi combat decoration).

Exaggerated reports of the size of the *Britische Freikorps* result from the fact that many (at least

Left *'Berry' and 'Minchen' outside the 'holiday camp'.* **Below** *The leaflet written by 'Wood' and circulated in PoW camps, plus 'Frank Wood's' SS identity book* (Christopher Ailsby Photographic Collection).

Fellow-Countrymen!

We of the British Free Corps are fighting for YOU!
We are fighting with the best of Europe's youth to preserve our European civilisation and our common cultural heritage from the menace of Jewish Communism.

MAKE NO MISTAKE ABOUT IT! Europe includes England. Should Soviet Russia ever overcome Germany and the other European countries fighting with her, nothing on this earth would save the Continent from Communism, and our own country would inevitably sooner or later succumb.

We are British. We love England and all it stands for. Most of us have fought on the battlefields of France, of Lybia, Greece, or Italy, and many of our best comrades in arms are lying there—sacrificed in this war of Jewish revenge. We felt then we were being lied to and betrayed. Now we know it for certain.

This conflict between England and Germany is racial SUICIDE. We must UNITE and take up arms against the common enemy. We ask you to join with us in our struggle. We ask you to come into our ranks and fight shoulder to shoulder with us for Europe and for England.

Published by the British Free Corps.

Fuzzy but recognisable details of the Freikorps collar patch and sleeve insignia (Christopher Ailsby Photographic Collection).

300) British PoWs accepted an invitation, or were ordered by their own officers to accept an invitation in order to gather information, to spend two or three weeks in a Berlin 'holiday camp'—actually an indoctrination and assessment centre. In the end, though, only 58 men became full members of the Freikorps and took to wearing Waffen-SS uniforms. Special distinctions included three embroidered leopards on the right-hand collar patch, a Union Jack shield on the lower left arm and a cuff title embroidered *'Britische Freikorps'* beneath the shield.

The first commanders of the *Freikorps* were the German Haupsturmführers Johannes Roggenfeld and Roepke, although who was actually in charge is hazy. (The author has commenced the research into a separate book on this subject and would welcome any information from readers.) Members of the Korps fought predominantly in Russia and, under their final commander (none other than Felix Steiner), were mostly captured by the Russians in Stettin whence they were returned to England for courts martial. A couple were captured in France and John Amery himself in Milan.

Amery pleaded guilty to the charge of treason and was executed, but others pleaded not guilty or refused to make any kind of statement and were sentenced to varying terms of imprisonment. At the time of writing it is believed there are ten survivors.

Right *'Eric Durin' (also spelt 'Duran'), the 'hard man' of the Freikorps.* **Below** *John Amery with his girlfriend after his capture in Milan* (Christopher Ailsby Photographic Collection).

2. Composition of a Waffen-SS Panzer Division, 1944

At full strength, a division comprised some 14-15,000 fighting men and 5-6,000 supporting troops—medical personnel, drivers, police, clerks, quartermasters and administrative staff, etc.

In June 1944, at the time of the Allied landings in Normandy, the following Waffen-SS Panzer Divisions were in existence:

I SS Panzer Division Leibstandarte *Adolf Hitler*;
II SS Panzer Division *Das Reich*;
III SS Panzer Division *Totenkopf*;
V SS Panzer Division *Wiking*;
IX SS Panzer Division *Hohenstaufen;*
X SS Panzer Division *Frundsberg*;
XII SS Panzer Division *Hitlerjugend.*

The basic composition of each was similar: one Panzer Regiment, two Panzergrenadier Regiments, a Panzer Artillery Regiment and flak, anti-tank, assault gun, reconnaissance, pioneer and signals battalions, plus supporting services.

The most important combat units in each division were as follows:

I—SS Panzer Regiment Nr 1, SS Panzergrenadier Regiment Nr 1 and SS Panzergrenadier Regiment Nr 2;
II—SS Panzer Regiment Nr 2, SS Panzergrenadier Regiment Nr 3 *Deutschland*, SS Panzergrenadier Regiment Nr 4 *Der Führer*;
III—SS Panzer Regiment Nr 3, SS Panzergrenadier Regiment Nr 5 *Thule*, SS Panzergrenadier Regiment Nr 6 *Theodor Eicke*;
V—SS Panzer Regiment Nr 5, SS Panzergrenadier Regiment Nr 9 *Germania*, SS Panzergrenadier Regiment Nr 10 *Westland*;
IX—SS Panzer Regiment Nr 9, SS Panzergrenadier Regiment Nr 19, SS Panzergrenadier Regiment Nr 20;
X—SS Panzer Regiment Nr 10, SS Panzergrenadier Regiment Nr 21, SS Panzergrenadier Regiment Nr 22;
XII—SS Panzer Regiment Nr 12, SS Panzergrenadier Regiment Nr 25, SS Panzergrenadier Regiment Nr 26.

Other divisions, although not designated Panzer Divisions, did include Panzer formations, as follows:

IV SS Polizei Panzergrenadier Division—SS Panzer Abteilung Nr 4;
XI Freiwilligen Panzergrenadier Division *Nordland*—SS Panzer Abteilung Nr 11 *Hermann von Salza*;
XVI SS Panzergrenadier Division *Reichsführer-SS*—SS Panzer Abteilung Nr 16;
XVIII SS Freiwilligen Panzergrenadier Division *Horst Wessel*—SS Panzer Abteilung Nr 18.

Tiger I and II tanks were not officially on the strengths of any of the divisions, being allotted to independent Heavy (Schwere) Panzer Battalions, eg, 501 schwere Panzer Abteilung which usually fought alongside the Leibstandarte *Adolf Hitler*.

At full strength, an SS Panzer Regiment comprised two battalions, each of four companies with an average of 15 tanks—PzKpfw IVs and Vs—to a company. In addition, each Panzer Regiment had a dozen or so light anti-aircraft guns—Möbelwagens, Wirbelwinds or Ostwinds—and an integral pioneer company, plus anything up to 350-400 motor cycles, cars and trucks, a total establishment of 1,700-2,000 men.

The Panzergrenadier Regiments were usually of three battalions, each of five companies equipped with SdKfz 251 half-tracks. They also included six 15 cm self-propelled artillery pieces (Hummels) and 12 10.5 cm pieces (Wespes), 24 flamethrower vehicles and 12 12 cm mortar carriers, plus 5-600 other vehicles. Full establishment was 3-4,000 men.

An SS Panzer Artillery Regiment typically comprised 12 batteries in four battalions, one battery in each battalion having self-propelled weapons and the remainder towed guns. For example, SS Panzer Artillery Regiment Nr 2 *(Das Reich)* had six Hummels, 12 Wespes, 12 17 cm K 18s, 12 15 cm sFH 18s and 12 10.5 cm leFH 18s. Establishment was 2,000 men plus.

The anti-aircraft battalions had five companies, two heavy and three light, each with six guns. In the heavy companies these were 8.8 cm weapons, in the light, 20 mm.

The anti-tank battalions had three companies, two with 15 self-propelled weapons—normally Jagdpanzer IVs—each, the third with towed 7.5 cm Pak 40s.

The assault gun battalions were surprisingly weak, comprising some 20 StuG IIIs/IVs in three companies, and only totalling some 300 men. The reconnaissance and pioneer battalions were much stronger, with nearly 1,000 men. The recce units included a dozen 7.5 cm self-propelled guns and both formations had integral light anti-tank and anti-aircraft weapons for self-defence.

Later in 1944, from September, Nebelwerfer battalions were added to the strengths of the SS Panzer Divisions. Each had four companies, one with three 21 cm mortars and the other three with 15 cm weapons. Some of these were on half-track chassis such as the Maultier.

3. Fate of the foreign divisions

The narrative in chapter 5 concentrates, through necessity, on the activities of the premier Waffen-SS formations, and it is therefore necessary here to summarise briefly the activities of the other units.

Prinz Eugen Except as described in the main text, this unit fought principally against Tito and, from October 1944, the Russians.

Nordland Virtually annihilated in Courland, the remnants fought to the death in the final defence of Berlin.

Handschar Mostly involved in anti-partisan operations in the Balkans. Surrendered to British troops in Austria.

Galizische (Ukrainische) Nr 1 Continued fighting against Soviets in the Carpathian Mountains until handed over to British in May 1945.

Lettische Nr 1 'Best fighting record of Baltic formations' according to Windrow (see bibliography). Finally surrendered to Russians; few survivors probable.

Lettische Nr 2 Not formed until early 1944 and suffered same fate as *Nr 1* above.

Estnische Nr 1 After heavy fighting in Russia from autumn 1944 onwards, suffered same fate as above two formations.

Skanderberg Useless formation, most deserted, final fate unknown.

Maria Theresia Did not see action until October 1944; annihilated in Budapest.

Niederlande (Nederland) Fought in Balkans late 1943 before transfer to Leningrad front; virtually wiped out in Courland but survivors fought with Steiner (see chapter 5) to the end. A tough bunch.

Karstjäger Mostly involved in anti-partisan activities in Italy; disintegrated and survivors presumably hid, joined other units, or were killed by old enemies.

Hunyadi After brief action against Soviet forces in the winter of 1944-45, survivors (not many) surrendered to Americans.

Ungarische Nr 2 No reliable information available.

Langemarck Fought well in Ukraine winter 1943-44; refitted in Czechoslovakia and thrown back in mêlée on Baltic coast; disintegrated.

Wallonien Cut off with *Wiking* in Cherkassy pocket *(qv)*; continued service after rest and refit on Eastern Front; this was Leon Dégrelle's unit, and fought well

Left *Sepp Dietrich (on left) watches while Leon Dégrelle presents medals to men of the 28th SS Division* Wallonien *in Charleroi during April 1944 following their escape from the Cherkassy pocket. Note that the Unterstumführer in the right foreground wears the rare Rex Treue Abzeichen and below it the Rex Bludordern, the party's highest decoration.* **Right** *Other members of the same division with their standards at the same ceremony* (Christopher Ailsby Photographic Collection).

Johannes Munk, from Leiden, was a Dutch volunteer in the SS. The close-up shows him during his first week as a recruit wearing the drill tunic without any insignia. The second picture shows him with a friend and two Gebirgsjäger just before they were sent to the Russian front. Munk distinguished himself by carrying his CO to safety, although wounded himself, and was rewarded by a commission to Bad Tölz (Christopher Ailsby Photographic Collection).

until finally split up and either decimated or captured.

Russische Nr 1 Interesting, if horrifying, one, this: formed from Russian prisoners of war by an entreprenurial character, Bronislav Kaminski; took up equivalent duties to earlier Einsatzgruppen and responsible for worst atrocities during suppression of Warsaw Uprising; Kaminski was killed, probably deliberately by his own troops, and the 'division' disintegrated.

Italienische Nr 1 Hardly existed except in name; some anti-partisan activity; honour number acquired from above unit.

Russische Nr 2 Took part in anti-Resistance operations in France during 1944 before being consigned to the Eastern Front and disappearing in the maelstrom.

Böhmen-Mähren Formed October 1944 and destroyed by Soviets early 1945.

30 Januar Formed from stragglers in Kurmark in January 1945 and virtually wiped out.

Ungarische Nr 3 Ad hoc cavalry force with no resemblance to a proper division, formed and destroyed in Hungary early 1945.

Charlemagne 'Fine record' as Army unit; when integrated into SS, fought in Balkans and Russia; some (presumably) stragglers known to have fought suicidally to the end in Berlin.

Landstorm Nederland Security operations in Holland, spring 1943-autumn 1944; steady retreat before Allies until surrender.

Polizei Grenadier Division No more than battalion strength and only formed, if that is the word, in February 1945.

Lützow Similar to above; formed from cavalry unit stragglers February-March 1945 and surrendered to Americans near Vienna.

Nibelungen Formed from young Hitler Youth candidates under training at Bad Tölz at the end of March 1945 and surrendered in Bavaria a month later; like most of the late war 'divisions', never even reached regimental size.

Other formations Dirlewanger and Skorzeny should at least be mentioned, but not really in the same breath. They both commanded penal units but the former's was composed of convicted criminals, particularly poachers and others with a knowledge of woodcraft, who committed unspeakable atrocities against the partisans in Russia and were responsible for some of the worst excesses during the suppression of the Warsaw uprising; while the latter only joined the SS because his stature was too large to enable him to do what he really wanted—join the Luftwaffe as a fighter pilot—and his SS Fallschirmjäger (men convicted of criminal or military offences while under arms but given a second chance) achieved a remarkable record, including the rescue of Mussolini from Gran Sasso and the impersonation of American soldiers during the Ardennes offensive.

Index